Ṣadr al-Di

his
Transcendent Theosophy

Background, Life and Works

by

Seyyed Hossein Nasr

Institute for Humanities
and
Cultural Studies

Tehran, 1997

Nasr, Hossein, 1933-

Ṣadr al-Dīn Shīrāzī and his transcendent theosophy, background, life and works / by Hossein Nasr. - 2nd. ed. - Tehran: Institute for Humanities and Cultural Studies, 1997.

155 p.: ill, facsims. - (Institute for Humanities and Cultural Studies; 75018)

First Published 1978 by Iranian Academy of Philosophy with series no. 29

Includes bibliographies.

1. Ṣadr al-Dīn Shīrāzī, Muḥammad ibn Ibrāhīm, 1571? - 1641. 2. Philosophy, Islamic. I. Title II. Series.

B 189.1

Institute for Humanities and Cultural Studies

Ṣadr al-Dīn Shīrāzī and His Transcendent Theosophy

First published 1978

Second edition *(With Additional Chapters)* Spring 1997

Production Manager: Mohammad Mehdi Dehghān

ISBN 978-964426-034-1

Publication No. 75018

Kazi Publications 3023 W. Belmont Avenue Chicago IL 60618

Table of Contents

بسم الله الرحمن الرحيم

In the Name of Allah – Most Merciful, Most Compassionate

Preface to the Second Edition

Nearly twenty has passed since the publication of the first edition of this work, during much of which time the book has been out of print. During this period, interest in Mullā Ṣadrā outside of Persia has grown from strength to strength. In the West hardly any general discussion of Islamic philosophy takes place these days without the name of Mullā Ṣadrā being mentioned and general histories of Islamic philosophy that have appeared during this period, such as the later edition of M. Fakhry's *A History of Islamic Philosophy* and S.H. Nasr and O. Leaman's *History of Islamic Philosophy*, have sections devoted to him. Moreover, numerous articles have appeared on his thought mostly in English and French and at least one of his works has been translated into English, namely the *Ḥikmat al-'arshiyyah* (by James Morris).

The studies on Mullā Ṣadrā carried out during the 1950's, 60's and 70's by H. Corbin, T. Izutsu, F. Rahman and ourselves have also led many students in various universities in both Europe and America to turn to a study of Mullā Ṣadrā. We ourselves have guided several doctoral and master's theses on the subject during the past few years and a number of Persian students at McGill University have written master's theses on various aspects of the teachings of Ṣadr al-Muta'allihīn during the past decade. It is of interest to note that some of these students are Muslims of countries other than Persia including the Arab world, Turkey, Indonesia and Malaysia. In this latter country the works of Mullā Ṣadrā are now taught in several institutions especially the International Institute of Islamic Thought and Civilization which has also brought out in its series of publications a work comparing the thought of Mullā Ṣadrā and Heidegger by A. Açikgenç from Turkey. There is likewise new interest in Egypt in Mullā Ṣadrā's work some of which have been printed there of late without awareness of current research going on in Persia while in

Pakistan and Muslim India much more attention is paid to him than before.

The translation of the present book into Turkish and Malay and its spread in the original English into many Muslim countries, especially Pakistan and Muslim India, have themselves played a humble role in the rise of interest in other Islamic countries in Mullā Ṣadrā's teachings, a renewal of interest which is perhaps more significant than the ever greater spread of his fame in the West. Corresponding to a deeply felt intellectual need at the present moment, the doctrines of the Master of Shiraz are in fact bound to continue to grow in both East and West as they have done during the past decades.

Needless to say, the most important research in the works of Mullā Ṣadrā during the last twenty years has been carried out in Persia itself, encouraged especially during the last few years by the organization established to commemorate his work and thought in the near future. The new dimensions revealed during this period are related on the one hand to his Quranic commentaries and on the other to certain aspects of his life and influence upon the formation of his thought. The tireless efforts of Muḥammad Khwājawī in editing, translating and elucidating the Quranic commentaries of Mullā Ṣadrā constitute the addition of a major chapter to the study of the Master's works. And then there are penetrating analyses of certain periods of his life such as the Qazwīn period and the formative influence upon him of the "School of Shiraz" comprised of such figures as Ghiyāth al-Dīn Manṣūr Dashtakī, Sayyid-i Sanad and Khafrī, by such scholars as Āyatullāh Sayyid Muḥammad Khāmini'ī. The results of all these avenues of research have enriched the whole domain of Ṣadrian studies and need to be incorporated in any future comprehensive study devoted to him.

Now that the *Transcendent Theosophy* is being reprinted in conjuction with the commemoration of Mullā Ṣadrā, the ideal would have been for us to re-write this book completely in the light of the above mentioned research. But such a possibility does not exist and meanwhile there has been much demand for a re-print of this work in the West. When asked by authorities concerned within the commemoration and especially Dr. M. Golshani and Dr. Gh. Aavani to have a new edition of the work to be printed in Persia, we decided instead of re-writing the whole text to add two chapters to the old edition, one dealing with the metaphysics of the Master and the other with the significance of his Quranic commentaries. Originally when we wrote the book twenty years ago, our hope was to publish a second volume devoted to his metaphysical and cosmological doctrine. Events which followed, leading to the loss of our library and notes, made that plan impossible. The present chapters are therefore a kind of compensation for the sequel to this work which has not been written. We hope, therefore, that in its new form the work will be more comprehensive and will serve as a more complete introduction to the life, works and teachings of Ṣadr al-Muta'allihīn.

Many in both the West and even Persia itself have criticized us as well as Corbin over the years for referring to *al-ḥikmat al-muta'āliyah* as the transcendent theosophy, rather than as meta-philosophy or something of the kind, in order to placate the expectations of academic Western philosophers many of whom have an instinctive aversion toward the term "theosophy". But as we have explained in many on our writings, one cannot use the term "philosophy" for both Quine and Mullā Ṣadrā in the same sense. Of course Mullā Ṣadrā's thought is philosophy as understood in the Islamic context, but it is also theosophy as understood by a Jacob Böhme and of course not modern occultists. With full awareness of the problem involved and determined to present Mullā Ṣadrā in a manner that conforms to the truth of his teachings and not simply for the sake of expediency, we have, therefore, decided to preserve the term theosophy as a translation of *ḥikmah* in the context of the *ḥikmat al-muta'āliyah*.

We hope that the new edition of this work will aid, as did the earlier edition, to make better known the remarkable synthesis of Mullā Ṣadrā between revelation, illumination and ratiocination in a world which is suffering so grievously as a result of its having separated these paths to the Truth from each other.

wa'Llāhu a'lam
Bethesda, Maryland
Rajab 1417 A.H. (L)
Aban 1375 A.H. (S)
November 1996 A.D.

Introduction to the First Edition

Although the classical view held in the West was that Islamic philosophy constituted a passing phenomenon and was merely a bridge between the late antiquity and the Latin high Middle Ages, gradually a wider perspective is becoming prevalent. Thanks to the writings and expositions of a small number of scholars writing in Western languages, the period during which over a millennium of Islamic philosophy was relegated to a short chapter entitled "Arabic philosophy" and inserted as a brief pause between "serious" periods of Western thought is now in many areas drawing to a close even if this change of view has not as yet become prevalent everywhere. The West has begun to become aware of other traditional civilizations as independent worlds worthy of consideration in their own right rather than only as stepping-stones towards the foundation and development of the modern West. Other traditional intellectual universes have begun to reveal themselves to those qualified to perceive them in all their grandeur, inner unity and at the same time rich diversity. In modern times, the West first turned to the metaphysical heritage of India and the Far East, although they are farther removed from its own heritage than the Islamic world,[1] but now gradually the same process is taking place in the case of Islam. For eight centuries since the translators of Cordova made the works of Islamic philosophers accessible to the Latin West, the view was held that Islamic philosophy (which was called Arabic philosophy[2] because of the language from which it was translated) consisted of the writings of a few men such as al-Kindī (Alkindus), al-Fārābī (Alfarabius), Ibn Sīnā (Avicenna), al-Ghazzālī (Algazel) and Ibn Rushd (Averroes) who simply transmitted the philosophy of Aristotle and the Neoplatonists to the West adding little of their own. It is now becoming an ever more widely recognized fact that the death of Averroes (595/1198), far from marking the end of Islamic philosophy, was simply the termination of one of its phases, and that for nearly eight centuries since Averroes wrote his famous commentaries upon Aristotle, Islamic philosophy has continued to possess a rigorous and rich life of its own centered mostly in Persia and the Indian sub-continent.

More than any other factor, the discovery of Ṣadr al-Dīn Shīrāzī (known usually as Mullā Ṣadrā) has been responsible for the new awareness in the West of the continued vitality of Islamic philosophy after the so-called medieval period.[3] While the name Mullā Ṣadrā (or sometimes even Ṣadrā) has been a household word in Persia, Afghanistan and the Indian subcontinent during the past centuries, he remained nearly completely unknown in the West until the beginning of this century. The only exceptions to this were a few passing references to him by European travellers to the East and the important pages devoted to him by Comte de Gobineau in his now classical *Les philosophies et les religions dans l'Asie centrale.*[4] Then during the early decades of this century, Muḥammad Iqbal, Edward G. Browne and Max Horten[5] turned the attention of the community of Islamicists in the West to him although the students of Islamic and medieval thought had as yet to awaken fully to the importance of his works.

It was only the discovery of Suhrawardī and through him of Mullā Ṣadrā by Corbin that finally provided the key for the serious introduction of Mullā Ṣadrā to both the orientalists and the philosophers in the West. When Corbin first journeyed to Persia after the Second World War in quest of the teachings of Suhrawardī, he was not aware of the rich philosophical tradition of the Safavid period to which the writings of the master of the school of Illumination (*ishrāq*) would naturally lead him. But soon he discovered a new world of metaphysics and traditional philosophy of men such as Mīr Dāmād and Mullā Ṣadrā to which he has devoted most of his energy during the past two decades.[6] Besides his numerous other studies on Mullā Ṣadrā, he is in fact still the only scholar to have translated a complete work of his into a European language.[7]

Following Corbin, the English writings of Toshihiko Izutsu[8] and our own humble works[9] have further spread the interest in Mullā Ṣadrā. Finally, last year the first book in English devoted completely to Mullā Ṣadrā saw the light of day. Written by the

Pakistani scholar, Fazlur Rahman, the book itself is the first fruit of the new interest which for the last fifteen years the works of the authors cited above have begun to awaken in him. This is now an interest shared by other scholars.[10] Moreover, numerous studies, translations and analyses of various aspects of the writings of Ṣadr al-Dīn are now under way in both Europe and America, as well as in the Islamic world and particularly in Persia where a major revival of interest in his works is under way.

* * *

The study of the writings of Mullā Ṣadrā presents certain difficulties which are not easy to surmount and which have driven many scholars away into less forbidding and more familiar fields of research. There is first of all the question of the availability of his writings. Until about fifteen years ago, only the most famous works such as the *Asfār* and *al-Shawāhid al-rubūbiyyah* were available in lithograph editions of such formidable character that to find the beginning of a particular chapter or discussion itself required long periods of study Thanks to the renewed interest in the writings of Mullā Ṣadrā during the past few years, a number of new editions have recently seen the light of day, corrected and edited by such scholars as 'Allāmah Ṭabāṭabā'ī, Sayyid Jalāl al-Dīn Āshtiyānī, Henry Corbin, S. H. Nasr and others, and all published in Persia. However, many of Mullā Ṣadrā's works remain either in manuscript form or in unsatisfactory editions. Even his most important *opus*, the *Asfār*, does not possess a critical edition despite the indefatigable efforts of 'Allāmah Ṭabāṭabā'ī who over a period of nearly ten years has edited nine volumes of this vast work.[11]

It is also important to recall the extensive nature of Mullā Ṣadrā's writings – over forty works covering thousands of pages and dealing with nearly every question of metaphysics, cosmology, eschatology, theology and related fields. As we shall see later in this study, the writings of Mullā Ṣadrā are devoted not only to traditional philosophy but also to Quranic commentary, *Ḥadīth*, and other religious sciences. Moreover, in the domain of traditional philosophy, they deal with not only one school of thought, but with the whole heritage of Islamic intellectual life. These factors, added to the innate difficulty of the doctrines involved, have made it well nigh impossible for scholars who are even specialists in Mullā Ṣadrā to have well-grounded knowledge of all of his writings. It takes nearly a lifetime to gain intimate knowledge of even one or two of his basic works. Practically no scholar, including most of all the author of these words, could claim to have carefully studied and mastered all of his works. For a long time, Ṣadrian studies will continue to be different glimpses of a vast mountain from different perspectives rather than an exhaustive survey of it. The more serious studies are those which penetrate in depth into certain aspects or particular works of the Master. One can hardly expect today a study which is at once profound and all embracing even by those who have spent a lifetime in the study in Mullā Ṣadrā.

Another major problem in the study of Mullā Ṣadrā in a manner which would be understandable and acceptable to the Western reader is his relation to the whole tree of the Islamic tradition of which he is a late fruit. It is of course possible to discuss Ṣadr al-Dīn's metaphysical ideas and doctrines in the light of their innate truth, but by and large the Western reader expects the author of these doctrines to be related to the traditional background from which he rose. Mullā Ṣadrā often quotes from a vast spectrum of authors – from the pre-Socratics, Pythagoras, Plato, Aristotle and Plotinus to the early Islamic philosophers, as well as from Sufis, the Illuminationists, theologians and religious authorities in the fields of Quran and *Ḥadīth*. One could and in fact should compose a separate work on Mullā Ṣadrā as a historian of ideas and philosophy. But even if one is not specifically concerned with this aspect of Mullā Ṣadrā,[12] one can hardly succeed in expounding the teachings of Mullā Ṣadrā without recourse to such figures as Ibn Sīnā, Suhrawardī, Ibn 'Arabī and Mīr Dāmād. Ideally, the writings of Mullā Ṣadrā should be expounded in the West only after scholars have elucidated fully the metaphysical and philosophical teachings of all of these and many other of the earlier masters of Islamic thought, a situation which is very far from being the case. Some of the figures, such as Ṣadr al-Dīn Dashtakī, who are quoted extensively by Mullā Ṣadrā are not known even to experts on Islamic philosophy in Persia.

A final problem in presenting the teachings of Mullā Ṣadrā is the question of language. Because Ibn Sīnā and other Peripatetics were translated into Latin, it is not difficult to develop an adequate vocabulary to discuss their works in modern European languages. The problem becomes more difficult with Suhrawardī and Ibn 'Arabī because for several centuries Western languages have been little concerned with metaphysical and gnostic doctrines of the order connected with the schools of these masters; in fact these schools have developed in quite the opposite direction. With Mullā Ṣadrā, the problem becomes even more difficult because of the total lack of precedents in expounding such doctrines in modern languages. There is a danger of reducing, through the use of inappropriate language, a doctrine of great metaphysical sublimity to a bland and harmless philosophical teaching, as the word "philosophical" is understood in its purely human and profane modern sense. To write of Mullā Ṣadrā's doctrines in English is to forge the container as well as to pour the contents from one vessel into another.

Despite all of those obstacles and problems, the teachings of Mullā Ṣadrā have to be and *can* be presented to the contemporary world. Since 1960, we have tried to achieve as much as possible through numerous studies in article and essay form written mostly in English.[13] Finally, as a result of the requests of many friends and students, we decided to write an extensive work on Mullā Ṣadrā which would serve to delineate the contours of this outstanding intellectual figure in relation to the vast panorama of the Islamic tradition and analyse the most important aspects of his doctrines. Several years of work enabled us to complete the first part of this project which concerns the life, the works, the relation of Mullā Ṣadrā to the totality of the Islamic tradition, and the characteristics of his "Transcendent Theosophy" (theosophy being used in its original sense and not according to its modern deformations). Other duties and obligations forced us to devote our intellectual energies to other projects and the book remained in its incomplete form while several of our other works saw the light of day. Finally, as a result of the prodding and insistence of friends, we decided to print the first part of this rather extensive study separately since it stands as an independent work. We hope to complete the second volume, which will deal with the metaphysics, theodicy, cosmology, epistemology, psychology and eschatology of Mullā Ṣadrā and the influence of his teaching.

In writing the present book, we have benefited as much and perhaps even more from the oral teaching we have received from the great expositors of the school of Mullā Ṣadrā in contemporary Persia, such men as the late Sayyid Muḥammad Kāẓim 'Aṣṣār, the late Mīrzā Sayyid Abu'l-Ḥasan Rafī'ī Qazwīnī, 'Allāmah Sayyid Muḥammad Ḥusayn Ṭabāṭabā'ī, the late Mīrza Mahdī Ilāhī Qumsha'ī and others,[14] as from the actual writings of the master. While we have had recourse to all the usual methods and techniques of scholarship, we have also relied heavily upon oral teachings which are extremely valuable and in fact indispensable while a tradition is still alive. The portrait of Mullā Ṣadrā presented in the following pages is, as much as possible, the one envisaged by men who have lived a lifetime with his teachings and who still breathe in the same spiritual universe which brought Mullā Ṣadrā into being and in which he lived and breathed. We are most grateful to these masters who considered us worthy to be taken into their intimacy and who taught us so much not to be found in books.

We want also to express our thanks to Dr. H. Sharifi and Dr. W. Chittick who have helped in so many ways with the printing of this work, to Mr. Ra'nā Ḥusaynī who provided the plates for the book and to Mrs. I. Hakemi and Mrs. C. Montagu for preparing this manuscript for the press.

wa mā tawfiqī illā bi'Llāh

Seyyed Hossein Nasr

Notes

1. One should perhaps say not in spite of their being far removed but because of it. These apparently more "exotic" universes of thought and discourse have attracted Westerners more readily than the Islamic world which appears too close to home for those who are in fact searching for these foreign worlds precisely because they want to move as far away as possible from their cultural and intellectual "homes".
2. Although there is logic in the use of the term "Arabic philosophy" by the Latin authors of the Middle Ages, there is no reason or excuse for the use of this term today. First, this philosophy is Islamic in the sense of being profoundly related to the intellectual and metaphysical principles of the Islamic revelation and cannot be justly described by any ethnic qualifiers. Secondly, if we wish to consider the ethnic groups which cultivated this philosophy, then the Persians, the Turks and the Muslims of the Indian subcontinent also had a major share in it. In fact, the largest number of Islamic philosophers were Persian and even according to the Arab historian Ibn Khaldūn, Persia was always the main home of Islamic philosophy. Finally, from the point of view of language, although Arabic is without doubt the most important language of Islamic philosophy, Persian is also of great significance and there are hundreds upon hundreds of works in

Persian on various themes of traditional philosophy. But beyond all those arguments, it should be mentioned that it is below the dignity of serious scholarship to succumb to parochial and passing waves of modern nationalism and that the term Islamic philosophy should be used for that vast intellectual heritage of all the Islamic peoples which in fact *is* Islamic philosophy.

3. So called, because this type of diversion does not apply to Islamic civilization where one finds "medieval" intellectual figures living in the nineteenth or even twentieth centuries.
4. See Comte de Gobineau, *Les religions et les philosophies dans l'Asie centrale*, Paris, 1866 and 1923.
5. Iqbal in his *Development of Metaphysics in Persia*, London, 1908, devoted much effort to expounding the writings of Sabziwārī, especially his *Asrār al-ḥikam*, but, since Sabziwārī is the commentator *par excellence* of Mullā Ṣadrā, this study naturally helped to focus attention upon Mullā Ṣadrā himself. Browne in the fourth volume of his monumental *A Literary History of Persia*, vol. IV, Cambridge, 1924, new edition 1969, pp. 429–32, also spoke of the sage from Shiraz and was instrumental in spreading his name although he knew little of his actual teachings.

   Max Horten was the first European to devote a complete work to Mullā Ṣadrā and in fact composed two separate books on him. See Horten, *Die Gottesbeweise bei Schirazi*, Bonn, 1912, and Horten, *Das philosophische System von Schirazi* (1640†), Strassburg, 1913. These works did not, however, receive as much attention as one would have expected.
6. On the intellectual life of Corbin and his discovery of Mullā Ṣadrā, see S.H. Nasr, 'The Life and Works of the Occidental Exile of Quest of the Orient of Light', *Sophia Perennis*, vol. III, no. 1, Spring, 1977, pp. 88–106. On the works of Corbin see S.H. Nasr (ed.), *Mélanges offerts à Henry Corbin*, Tehran, 1977, pp. iii–xxxii.
7. See Corbin, *Le livre des pénétrations métaphysiques*, Tehran-Paris, 1964, which contains the French translation of Mullā Ṣadrā's major epitome of ontology, the *Kitāb al-mashā'ir*.
8. See especially his *The Concept and Reality of Existence*, Tokyo, 1971.
9. See S.H. Nasr, *Islamic Studies*, Beirut, 1966; "Mullā Ṣadrā" in the *Encyclopedia of Philosophy*; and S.H. Nasr (ed.), *Mullā Ṣadrā Commemoration Volume*, Tehran, 1380/1961.
10. See Fazlur Rahman, *The Philosophy of Mullā Ṣadrā*, Albany (N.Y.), 1977.

    This book, although quite scholarly, is based completely on a more or less "rationalistic" interpretation of the writings of Mullā Ṣadrā without recourse to the living oral tradition connected with his school and without consideration of the intellectual and spiritual background from which he rose or of the gnostic and mystical elements which are essential to his teachings.
11. The faults of the new edition, which are many, must be placed upon the shoulders of the publishers rather than the editor. The publishers did not spend the necessary effort and care in correcting proofs and in providing the necessary indexes which would open the innumerable riches of this work to the uninitiated reader.
12. See S.H. Nasr, "Mullā Ṣadrā as a Source for the History of Islamic Philosophy", in Nasr, *Islamic Studies*, chapter eleven.
13. See the works cited in footnote 9 as well as Nasr, "Mullā Ṣadrā" in M.M. Sharif (ed.), *A History of Muslim Philosophy*, vol. II, Wiesbaden, 1966, pp. 1316–32.
14. On these venerable masters with all of whom we had the good fortune of being able to study for many years see S.H. Nasr, *Islamic Philosophy in Contemporary Persia: A Survey of Activity during the Past Two Decades*, Salt Lake City (Utah, U.S.A.), 1972, pp. 6–7.

Chapter 1

The Intellectual Background

The appearance of an intellectual figure of the dimensions of Ṣadr al-Dīn Shīrāzī during the Safavid period indicates the presence of a strong living intellectual tradition whose deepest currents he was to bring so brilliantly to the surface. Mullā Ṣadrā (as he is usually called) is a metaphysician and sage of outstanding stature who cannot be taken in isolation and separated from the tradition that produced him. The historical and philosophical research of the past twenty years has only now begun to reveal some of the features of this intellectual tradition to which Mullā Ṣadrā belonged.[1] A few of the peaks have been made known but literally hundreds of major works of a gnostic (*'irfānī*), theosophical and philosophical nature remain to be unearthed and made available in printed form. Until this is accomplished, it is not possible to know in detail the chain that connects Mullā Ṣadrā to the older masters of Islamic philosophy and theology such as Fārābī, Ibn Sīnā and Ghazzālī.

The tree is, however, judged by the fruit it bears, and even if we do not as yet know all the branches of the tree we can judge from the fruit the nature of the long tradition that finally produced Mullā Ṣadrā. In order to learn something of this tradition we must go back a few centuries to the fourth/tenth and fifth/eleventh centuries when the early phase of Islamic intellectual life reached its peak both in philosophy with Ibn Sīnā and in Sufism and theology with those masters of the Seljuq period like Khwājah 'Abdallāh Anṣārī and Sanā'ī in Sufism and Imām al-Ḥaramayn Juwaynī in *kalām* or theology. The teachings of these early masters of Sufism and *kalām* have become a permanent heritage of the Islamic world, perhaps most of all through the writings of Ghazzālī.

This early period of Islamic intellectual history is much better known than the later epoch with which we are concerned. We know how the Peripatetic (*mashshā'ī*) school reached its early phase of maturity with Ibn Sīnā and continued during the fifth/eleventh century with his immediate disciples like Bahmanyār and Juzjānī. We also know that at this time the political centralization brought about by the Seljuqs and the re-strengthening of the Abbasid caliphate combined with the spread of the Niẓāmiyyah *madrasah* system favored the study of *kalām* over philosophy and brought into being a period of nearly two centuries during which the center of the intellectual stage was occupied by theologians of great stature and acumen who severely attacked philosophy. Some like Ghazzālī were also Sufis and others like Fakhr al-Dīn Rāzī were first and last theologians.[2]

It is the later phase of the intellectual life of Islam, especially in the eastern lands of *dār al-islām*, that is not as well known and remains a *terra incognita* waiting to be explored. The West still accepts the view that Ghazzālī in the *Tahāfut al-falāsifah* (*The Incoherence of the Philosophers*), put an end to philosophy in Islam except in Andalusia where it survived for some time through the influence of Ibn Rushd.[3] Unfortunately, despite all the evidence that has been discovered during the last decades, this fallacious view continues to be taught in both the West and in those Muslim universities where the concept of Islamic philosophy is adopted from Occidental sources.[4]

What remains much less known, however, is the revival of Islamic intellectual life in the eastern lands of Islam, especially in Persia. During the sixth/twelfth and seventh/thirteenth centuries, this was made possible by the establishment of new intellectual schools by Suhrawardī and Ibn 'Arabī, followed by the resurrection of Ibn Sīnā's teachings during the middle decades of the seventh/thirteenth century by Khwājah Naṣīr al-Dīn Ṭūsī. The background of Mullā Ṣadrā must be sought in these schools as well as in the Sunni and Shi'ite schools of *kalām* as they developed from the seventh/thirteenth to the tenth/sixteenth centuries.

The four classical schools of the post-Mongol period, namely, the Peripatetic (*mashshā'ī*). the Illuminationist (*ishrāqī*), the gnostic (*'irfānī*) and the theological (*kalām*), with all the inner variations contained in each of them, developed extensively during the four centuries preceding Mullā Ṣadrā and also approached each other, preparing the ground for the major synthesis brought about by Mullā Ṣadrā. To understand the background of Mullā Ṣadrā, it is necessary to delve into the development of each of these schools as well as the interactions that occurred between them during this very rich and at the same time most neglected period of Islamic intellectual life, from the seventh/thirteenth through the tenth/sixteenth centuries.

Let us begin with the Peripatetic school. The works of the earlier masters of this school, especially those of the outstanding spokesman of the Muslim Peripatetics, Ibn Sīnā, underwent a thorough criticism and attack at the hands of both Sufis and theologians. The Sufis such as Sanā'ī and Rūmī criticized in a general way the rationalistic tendencies of the human mind and the attempt made by the philosophers to reach Divine Knowledge with the help of the Aristotelian syllogism. Certain theologians like Ghazzālī made the attack more pointed by selecting specific topics which they analyzed and refuted with the claim that these views went against the tenets of religion. Or they chose specific works of the philosophers which they likewise sought to criticize through textual analysis. This last method was carried out by Fakhr al-Dīn Rāzī, who chose the last masterpiece of Ibn Sīnā, the *al-Ishārāt wa'l-tanbīhāt* (*The Book of Directives and Remarks*) for detailed criticism, analyzing every page and nearly every word and phrase.

During the seventh/thirteenth century, Naṣīr al-Dīn Ṭūsī revived the school of Ibn Sīnā by answering these attacks, especially in his *Sharḥ al-ishārāt* (*Commentary upon the Directives and Remarks*), which is a landmark in the revival of *mashshā'ī* philosophy. This monumental work matches Ibn Sīnā's own writings as an authoritative source for the doctrines of this school. Naṣīr al-Dīn also wrote many works of his own following the teachings of Ibn Sīnā. Nor was he alone in this undertaking. His friend and contemporary, Najm al-Dīn Dabīrān Kātibī, composed a major treatise of *mashshā'ī* thought, the *Ḥikmat al-'ayn* (*Wisdom of the Fountainhead*), and Athīr al-Dīn Abharī wrote the *Kitāb al-hidāyah* (*The Book of Guidance*), both of which remain to this day favorite texts of Peripatetic philosophy and are taught in many *madrasahs*. Naṣīr al-Dīn's own students and colleague, Quṭb al-Dīn Shīrāzī, although not only a Peripatetic philosopher, wrote the voluminous philosophical encyclopedia *Durrat al-tāj* (*The Jewel of the Crown*) in Persian, following the model of the *Shifā'* (*The

Book of Remedy) of Ibn Sīnā, while his student, Quṭb al-Dīn Rāzī, wrote his *Muḥākamāt* (*Trials*) as a "trial" between the commentaries of Fakhr al-Dīn Rāzī and Naṣīr al-Dīn Ṭūsī upon the *Ishārāt*.

Meanwhile, from the eighth/fourteenth century onward Shiraz and its surroundings became the center of philosophy. Jalāl al-Dīn Dawānī followed Naṣīr al-Dīn's example in composing a work on philosophical ethics in Persian, the *Akhlāq-i jalālī* (*The Jalālī Ethics*), based on the earlier *Akhlāq-i nāṣirī* (*The Nasirean Ethics*) of Ṭūsī and also wrote several Peripatetic treatises as well as works on theology and illumination. The Dashtakī family produced some brilliant figures, foremost among them Ṣadr al-Dīn Dashtakī and Ghiyāth al-Dīn Manṣūr Dashtakī, both of whom exercised immense influence on Safavid thinkers as well as on the Muslim intellectual figures of the subcontinent, the latter group mostly through Fatḥallāh Shīrāzī. The writings of the Dashtakī family have not been edited at all, despite the presence of many fine manuscripts of their works in the subcontinent, Persia and Turkey. But they are without doubt among the most important predecessors of Mullā Ṣadrā.

As for the *ishrāqī* school, it was founded by Shaykh al-ishrāq Shihāb al-Dīn Suhrawardī,[5] who despite a short life of thirty eight lunar years established a new intellectual perspective and exercised an immense influence in the eastern lands of Islam and especially upon Mullā Ṣadrā. Suhrawardī created a theosophy based on illumination but also in a certain sense based upon Ibn Sīnā's philosophy. He also created an isthmus between discursive thought and mystical intuition. The school founded by him soon found capable followers and commentators. Shams al-Dīn Shahrazūrī, his foremost biographer, also wrote the first outstanding commentary upon his masterpiece, the *Ḥikmat al-ishrāq* (*The Theosophy of the Orient of Light*), soon to be followed by Quṭb al-Dīn Shīrāzī, whose commentary upon the same work is better known than that of Shahrazūrī. Dawānī, although of Peripatetic tendency, commented upon Suhrawardī's *Hayākil al-nūr* (*The Temples of Light*) while even Naṣīr al-Dīn before him was influenced in certain aspects of his thought by Suhrawardī. Mullā Ṣadrā was deeply cognizant of this tradition and in fact wrote glosses upon Quṭb al-Dīn's commentary of the *Ḥikmat al-ishrāq*.

When we come to consider gnosis or '*irfān*, the seventh/thirteenth century marks a golden age and a kind of return to the beginning of Islam and its spiritual intensity.[6] Such spiritual giants as Ibn 'Arabī, Ṣadr al-Dīn Qunyawī, and Jalāl al-Dīn Rūmī were nearly contemporaries. It is, however, especially the Sufism of the school of Ibn 'Arabī with its doctrinal and highly intellectual form that was of great influence upon Mullā Ṣadrā.[7] Through Ibn 'Arabī's immediate disciple, Ṣadr al-Dīn Qunyawī, as well as through his doctrinal commentators such as Sa'd al-Dīn Farghānī, Mu'ayyid al-Dīn Jandī, 'Abd al-Razzāq Kāshānī, Dā'ūd Qayṣarī and 'Abd al-Raḥmān Jāmī, this school developed a very elaborate metaphysics without which the whole doctrine of Mullā Ṣadrā is incomprehensible. Likewise, the Persian Sufi poets and authors such as Rūmī, Fakhr al-Dīn 'Arāqī, Sa'd al-Dīn Ḥamūyah, 'Azīz al-Dīn Nasafī, Awḥad al-Dīn Kirmānī, Maḥmūd Shabistarī and again Jāmī, not to speak of his own compatriot Ḥāfiẓ, were known to Mullā Ṣadrā and exercised much influence upon him. His citation of Persian Sufi poetry reveals how intimately he was acquainted with both the doctrinal school of *'irfān,* most of whose works are in Arabic, and the Persian Sufi literature that was inspired by it. It also shows how well he knew other schools of Sufism such as that of Central Asia associated with the name of Najm al-Dīn Kubrā.

As for *kalām,* both Sunni and Shi'ite theology underwent an important phase of development at this time. As far as Sunni *kalām* is concerned, the centuries immediately preceding Mullā Ṣadrā represent a major creative phase after Fakhr al-Dīn Rāzī, during which the works of such men as Qāḍī 'Aḍud al-Dīn Ījī, Sa'd al-Dīn Taftāzānī and Sayyid Sharīf Jurjānī were produced, codifying *kalām* in a form that continued until the advent of Shāh Waliallāh in the twelfth/eighteenth century in the subcontinent and in fact that continues to be taught to this day in many Sunni schools.

Shi'ite *kalām* in its systematic form was born during this period. The earlier masters from the fourth/tenth century onward such as Muḥammad ibn Ya'qūb Kulaynī, Ibn Bābūyah, Shaykh Muḥammad al-Ṭūsī and Aḥmad ibn 'Alī Ṭabarsī had made available the sources for theological meditation. It was, however, Naṣīr al-Dīn Ṭūsī who with his *Tajrīd* produced the first systematic work on Shi'ite *kalām,* to be followed by his student 'Allāmah Ḥillī and many other scholars who at this time hailed mostly from Ḥillah and the Jabal 'Āmil. In fact, a very large number of commentaries and glosses were written upon the *Tajrīd* before Mullā Ṣadrā, from that of Ḥillī to the glosses of Fakhrī and of others who belonged to the period one or two generations before Sadr al-Dīn. These commentaries, still for the most part neglected, from the borderline between theology and philosophy and contain in themselves four centuries' history of an important aspect of Islamic thought.

It was at this time that the four schools of thought mentioned above were penetrating Shi'ite thinking, a very significant phenomenon that prepared the ground for the Safavid renaissance with its specifically Shi'ite color. During this period, while Ismā'īlism went more or less underground following the fall of Alamut, twelve-imam Shi'ism began to produce its first monumental theosophical works. The foremost figure of this period is Sayyid Ḥaydar Āmulī, who sought to harmonize Sufism and Shi'ism and to show their essential unity, a theme which forms the basis of his major *opus, Jāmi' al-asrār* (*The Sum of Divine Mysteries*). But he was also a commentator of the *Fuṣūṣ al-ḥikam* (*Bezels of Wisdom*) of Ibn 'Arabī and represents an important instance of the remarkable process whereby the teachings of Ibn 'Arabī became absorbed into the intellectual perspective of Shi'ism.

Sayyid Ḥaydar Āmulī was not the only figure in this process, although perhaps the most important one. There were other noteworthy Shi'ite theologians with gnostic tendencies such as Rajab Bursī and especially Ibn Abī Jumhūr Aḥsā'ī, whose *Kitāb al-mujlī* (*The Book of the Source of Illumination*) is again a Shi'ite interpretation of the Sufism of Ibn 'Arabī. Likewise, some Shi'ite theologians turned towards *ishrāqī* and *mashshā'ī* philosophy and some tried to harmonize them, as we see in the case of Ṣā'in al-Dīn ibn Turkah Iṣfahānī, author of *Tamhīd al-qawā'id* (*The Preparation of Principles*), who was the first person to synthesise the teachings of Ibn Sīnā, Suhrawardī and Ibn 'Arabī, thereby anticipating in a certain way the achievement of Mullā Ṣadrā.

During the period stretching from the Mongol invasion to the establishment of the Safavid regime, we thus see on the one hand a development of the classical Islamic intellectual schools and on the other attempts to bring these schools together. During this period it is possible to observe all kinds of combinations of these schools. Some like Dawānī are both theologians and philosophers; others like Sayyid Sharīf Jurjānī are both theologians and Sufis, while yet others like Quṭb al-Dīn Shīrāzī and Ibn Turkah are well versed in the Peripatetic, Illuminationist and Sufi schools. Through the development of each of these disciplines as well as their interplay, the ground was prepared for the Safavid renaissance and the synthesis brought about by Mullā Ṣadrā.

The immediate background of Mullā Ṣadrā is to be found in the first generation of Safavid sages, who finally prepared the stage for his vast intellectual synthesis. With the coming of the Safavids, the state religion of Persia became Shīʿism, and Shīʿite scholars, brought from many places including Bahrayn, Iraq and Jabal ʿĀmil in the Lebanon, soon strengthened Persian Shīʿite centers of learning and caused the religious sciences to flourish. Such families as Jazāʾirī, Shūshtarī and ʿĀmilī produced many an illustrious figure in the religious and intellectual sciences. The revival of Shīʿism itself made possible the renaissance of the intellectual sciences (*al-ʿulūm al-ʿaqliyyah*) because they had been intimately linked with the Shīʿite dimension of Islam from the early centuries of Islamic history.[8]

Of course a certain amount of tension between the scholars of the exoteric sciences and the sages (*ḥukamāʾ*) continued and is reflected in Mullā Ṣadrā's autobiographical treatise, the *Sih aṣl* (*The Three Principles*). This was an inevitable consequence of the presence of a philosophy that had turned toward Sufism and gnosis and had gained an esoteric color. But the revival of this theosophy, or *ḥikmat-i ilāhī* as it has been known in Persia and the subcontinent, was not in spite of Shīʿism but because of it, notwithstanding the difficulties caused in certain cases by the exoteric authorities. The connection between this *ḥikmat-i ilāhī* and the Shīʿite vision of the Universe is too deeply rooted to be disregarded. There is a causal link between them, although Shīʿism, because it possessed an exoteric as well as esoteric aspect and had become the official state religion, reacted to a certain extent in its exoteric aspect against some of the purely esoteric formulations of theosophy such as the transcendent unity of being (*waḥdat al-wujūd*). This reaction was similar to that which has been observed in Sunni circles among some of the jurisprudents (*fuqahāʾ*). But it was also Shīʿism which integrated this theosophy into the curriculum of its *madrasahs*, so that to this day traditional theosophy and philosophy are taught in such schools, and the traditional masters of Islamic philosophy are for the most part products of these schools.

Moreover, the structure of this theosophy is linked in general in a most intimate manner with Islamic esotericism. Without the inspiration and spiritual vision that can come only from the esoteric dimension of Islam, this theosophy could never have come into being or been able to resuscitate in the light of a living gnosis the sapiential doctrines of the ancients.

In the tenth/sixteenth century, within the bosom of the new Shi'ite atmosphere of Persia, a series of outstanding philosophers and theosophers appeared, some of whom were the teachers of Mullā Ṣadrā. A few of these figures have not been studied at all, until now, while others like Mīr Dāmād, Mīr Findiriskī, Shaykh Bahā' al-Dīn 'Āmilī and Sayyid Aḥmad 'Alawī are very famous at least in the East, although most of even their works have not been fully studied. Among these figures Mīr Dāmād is especially important as the founder of the "School of Isfahan" in which Mullā Ṣadrā was trained.

Mīr Muḥammad Bāqir Dāmād, about whom we shall have occasion to speak more fully in the next chapter, was the son-in-law (*dāmād* in Persian) of Muḥaqqiq-i Karakī, one of the foremost Shi'ite theologians of the early Safavid period; hence the title Mīr Dāmād. Protected by the religious authority of his father-in-law and being himself both a master of the religious sciences and a person of great piety, Mīr Dāmād was able to light once again the torch of traditional philosophy in Isfahan and at the same time to stave off the possible criticism of some of the exoteric authorities. He brought to life a Suhrawardian interpretation of Avicennan philosophy, about which he wrote many books and which he taught to a generation of students in Ispahan, among them Mullā Ṣadrā.

When the young Mullā Ṣadrā came to Isfahan, he entered a climate where the intellectual sciences could be pursued alongside the "transmitted" or religious sciences (*al-'ulūm al-naqliyyah*) and where there were in fact masters who were authorities in both domains. This was due most of all to Mīr Dāmād, but the other outstanding figures of this era such as Mīr Findiriskī and Shaykh Bahā' al-Dīn 'Āmilī also shared this distinction. The Ispahan of Mullā Ṣadrā's day, and also to a large extent his own Shiraz and other major cities of Persia, were now able to provide a traditional education where, within the matrix of Shi'ite religious studies, *ḥikmat-i ilāhī* could also be studied and mastered. Most of the teachers of this "divine science" were in Ispahan but other cities were not completely deprived of them, least of all Shiraz.

When, therefore, we look back upon the intellectual background of Mullā Ṣadrā, we observe nine centuries of Islamic theology, philosophy and Sufism which had developed as independent disciplines in the earlier centuries and which gradually approached each other after the seventh/thirteenth century, becoming steadily more integrated within the matrix of Shi'ism. Mullā Ṣadrā was an heir to this vast intellectual treasure and was fully conscious of its doctrines, methods and problems. He thought and lived with questions such as the relation between faith and reason that had occupied Muslim thinkers from the early Mu'tazilites and al-Kindī onward. He meditated upon metaphysical and cosmological problems within an intellectual space whose dimensions were dominated by such figures as Ibn Sīnā, Ghazzālī, Suhrawardī and Ibn 'Arabī.

Mullā Ṣadrā studied his past fervently, not as a dead past, but as permanent intellectual perspectives that continued to be relevant within the living tradition of Islam. Having absorbed these teachings thoroughly, he then set about to create a synthesis and a new intellectual dimension, the "transcendent theosophy" (*al-ḥikmat al-muta'āliyah*), which was not just an eclecticism, a putting together of different theories and views, but a new school based upon a fresh interpretation of the traditional verities. It was a school that was at once new and traditional, such as can be produced only by a veritable reviver (*mujaddid*) of traditional teachings, who is able to renovate a doctrine because of a new and fresh vision of the transcendent truths which the traditional doctrines reveal and expound. Mullā Ṣadrā was such a *mujaddid*; through the prism of his luminous intellect a new intellectual perspective was born which was at once profoundly Islamic and attuned to both the logical demands of the mind and the requisites of the spiritual vision that is made possible through the opening of the "eye of the heart" (the *'ayn al-qalb* or *chishm-i dil*). Mullā Ṣadrā possessed that rare combination of perfect religious faith, acutely logical mind and a "heart" inclined by nature towards the contemplation of the supernal verities that made possible the founding of a school such as that of the "transcendent theosophy". He created a body of teachings in which the theological, philosophical, mystical and gnostic schools in Islam were at last harmonized after they had undergone their full elaboration.

Seen in this light, Mullā Ṣadrā represents one of the crowning achievements of nearly a millennium of intellectual life and restates in an explicit and outwardly manifested form the Unity that dominates the Islamic message and has been implicit and ever present from the very beginning of the Islamic revelation in all the true expressions of Islamic intellectuality.

Notes

1. Foremost among scholars who have studied the few centuries preceding Mullā Ṣadrā is Henry Corbin, who has devoted many monographs to the period between Suhrawardī and Mullā Ṣadrā and has also edited a major text (with Osman Yahia) of Sayyid Ḥaydar Āmulī which belongs to this period. See Sayyed Haydar Amoli, *La philosophie shi'ite*, ed. by H. Corbin and O. Yahia, Tehran-Paris, 1969. This large volume contains the Arabic text of *Jāmi' al-asrār*, which is a major document of the intellectual tradition preceding Mullā Ṣadrā. There is also an important introduction on the author and his influence.

   Other works concerned with the centuries preceding Mullā Ṣadrā include Muṣṭafā Kāmil al-Shaybī, *al-Ṣilah bayn al-taṣawwuf wa'l-tashayyu'*, 2 vols., Baghdad, 1963–64; al-Shaybī, *al-Faikr al-shī'ī wa'l-naẓa'āt al-ṣūfiyyah*, Baghdad, 1966; S.H. Nasr, *Three Muslim Sages*, Cambridge (Mass.), 1964 and Albany, 1976; S.H. Nasr, *Islamic Studies*, Beirut, 1966; S.H. Nasr, "Suhrawardī" in M.M. Sharif (ed.), *A History of Muslim Philosophy*, Wiesbaden, 1963, pp. 372–98; Ṣadr al-Dīn Shīrāzī, *Risālah si aṣl*, Tehran, 1340 (A.H. solar), introduction by S.H. Nasr.
2. We have dealt with this theme in several of our writings. See for example, Nasr, *Three Muslim Sages*, Chapter I.
3. Even this early period of Islamic philosophy is usually studied without taking into consideration all its richness. See H. Corbin (with the collaboration of S.H. Nasr and O. Yahya), *Histoire de la philosophie islamique*, vol. I, Paris, 1964).
4. See S.H. Nasr, *Islamic Studies*, Chapters 8 and 9.
5. Concerning Suhrawardī see the three prolegomena of H. Corbin to *Opera Metaphysica et Mystica* of Suhrawardī, vol. I, Tehran, 1976; vol. II, Tehran, 1977; vol. III, Tehran, 1977, the first two volumes edited by Corbin and the third by S.H. Nasr. These are new editions of these volumes which had appeared earlier in Istanbul and Tehran-Paris. See also S.H. Nasr, *Three Muslim Sages*, chapter II; Nasr, "Suhrawardī" in M.M. Sharif, op. cit.; and Nasr's Persian preface to *Majmū'ay-i āthār-i fārsī-yi Suhrawardī* (*Opera Metaphysica et Mystica*, vol. III). See also Corbin, *En Islam iranien*, vol. II, Paris 1972; and his *Sohravardi, L'Archange empourpré*, Paris, 1976.
6. This important question, which concerns the "return" of a tradition to its golden age during a particular phase of its development, which is also a "fall" from its origin, has been discussed by F. Schuon in several of his works. See, for example, his *In the Tracks of Buddhism*, trans. Marco Pallis, London, 1968, p. 153; and *Islam and the Perennial Philosophy*, trans. J.P. Hobson, London, 1976, pp. 25–26.

   For a general but penetrating treatment of this question see also his *Light on the Ancient Worlds*, trans. by Lord Northbourne, London, 1965.
7. On Ibn 'Arabī see T. Burckhardt, *La sagesse des prophètes*, Paris, 1955 and 1976; Corbin, *L'imagination créatrice dans le soufisme d'Ibn 'Arabī*, Paris, 1977; T. Izutsu, *A Comparative Study of the Key Philosophical Concepts in*

Sufism and Taoism – Ibn 'Arabī *and Lao-Tzu, Chuang-Tzu,* Part One, Tokyo, 1966; Nasr, *Three Muslim Sages,* Chapter III.

8. On the relation between Shī'ism and the intellectual sciences see S.H. Nasr, *Science and Civilization in Islam,* New York, 1970, introduction; and S.H. Nasr, *An Introduction to Islamic Cosmological Doctrines,* London, 1978, introduction.
9. Concerning Mīr Dāmād and the school of Ispahan see H. Corbin, "Confessions extatiques de Mīr Dāmād", *Mélanges Louis Massignon,* Damascus, 1956, pp. 331–78; his "Mīr Dāmād et l'Ecole Théologique d'Ispahan au XVIIe Siècle", *Etudes Carmélitaines,* 1960, pp. 53–71; Corbin, *En Islam iranien,* vol. IV, Paris, 1973, pp. 9–53; S.H. Nasr, "The School of Ispahan", in M.M. Sharif (ed.), *A History of Muslim Philosophy,* vol. II, Wiesbaden, 1966, pp. 904–32. We have dealt with the general history of philosophy, theology and Sufism in the Safavid period in a long chapter that is to appear in volume six of the *Cambridge History of Iran.* No extensive monographic study has as yet been published on Mīr Dāmād. S. 'Alī Mūsawī Bihbahānī, S.I. Dībājī and M. Muḥaqqiq (Mohaghegh) are preparing the critical edition of his *Qabasāt,* which will be the first of his works to have a modern critical edition.

   On the background of Mullā Ṣadrā see also the two introductions of Sayyid Jalāl al-Dīn Āshtiyānī to Mullā Ṣadrā's *al-Shawāhid al-rubūbiyyah,* Mashhad, 1346 (A.H. solar), *Sharḥ risālat al-mashā'ir* of Mullā Ṣadrā by Mullā Muḥammad Ja'far Lāhījānī (Langarūdī), 1384/1964, and several other studies contained in various introductions to his works cited in the next chapter.

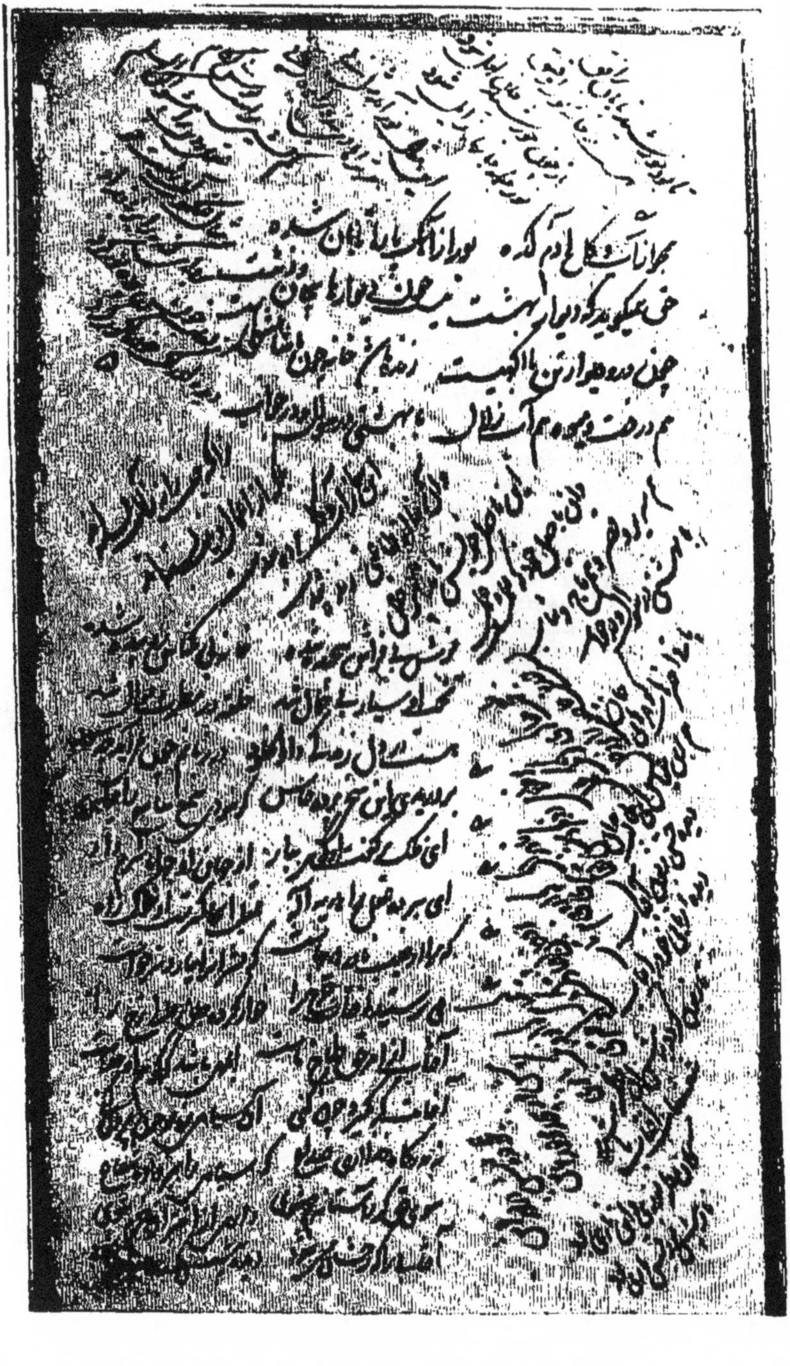

A section of the *Mathnawī* of Jalāl al-Dīn Rūmī in the handwriting of Mullā Ṣadrā

Chapter 2

Life and Works

Life

Muḥammad ibn Ibrāhīm ibn Yaḥyā Qawāmī Shīrāzī, entitled Ṣadr al-Dīn and also Mullā Ṣadrā (in the Indo-Pakistani subcontinent simply Ṣadrā) as well as Ṣadr al-muta'allihīn, "foremost among the theosophers", or called simply Ākhūnd by his disciples, was born in Shiraz in 979–980/1571–72 into an influential and well known family, his father having been the governor of the province of Fars. The date of his birth has not been specified in any of the traditional sources devoted to him[1] and in fact it was discovered only a few years ago when 'Allāmah Sayyid Muḥammad Ḥusayn Ṭabāṭabā'ī, a foremost contemporary sage or *ḥakīm* of Iran, was correcting the new edition of the *Asfār* and preparing it for publication. On the margin of a manuscript copied in 1197/1703 but based on a copy autographed by Mullā Ṣadrā and with certain marginal notes by the author himself, 'Allāmah Ṭabāṭabā'ī discovered the following sentence in the section devoted to the question of the unity of the intellect and the intelligible: "I received this inspiration at the time of sunrise of Friday the seventh of Jumādī al-ūlā of the year 1037 A.H. [corresponding to January 14, 1628] when already 58 lunar years had passed from the life of the author."[2] Since then other sources have confirmed this information. But because it is not possible to know whether the 58 years is a period of between 57 and 58 years or 58 complete years, one cannot determine the exact date of his birth beyond setting it between the years 979/1571 and 980/1572.

Being the only male child of a well-to-do family which had prayed long to be given a male descendant, he was brought up with the greatest care and provided with the best education possible in his city of birth. Shiraz had for centuries before the rise of the Safavids been the center of Islamic philosophy and other traditional disciplines, a center which was still alive in the tenth/sixteenth century although functioning less vigorously than before. The early period of training of Mullā Ṣadrā was in this tradition of learning. He was a precocious child, able to master rapidly all that was taught him. He displayed from the earliest age a profound piety combined with keen intelligence. He was soon able to master the religious sciences as well as all to which he could gain access in the field of the "intellectual sciences". With a firm knowledge of Arabic and Persian, the Quran and *Ḥadīth,* and an elementary training in the other Islamic disciplines, he now set out to expand further his intellectual horizons. He was not able to remain satisfied for long with what Shiraz could offer him. After benefiting to the extent possible from the lessons of the teachers of that city, he therefore set out for Isfahan, which in the field of philosophy had by now become the major intellectual center of Persia and perhaps of the whole Islamic East. The date of his departure for Isfahan is unknown, like nearly all other dates of his life except for those of his birth and death. But it is certain that he was still a very young man, a student, albeit an advanced one.

Isfahan did not disappoint him, for there he found several outstanding masters who influenced him profoundly. Mullā Ṣadrā studied with both Shaykh Bahā' al-Dīn 'Āmilī and Mīr Dāmād and also possibly with Mīr Abu'l-Qāsim Findiriskī in the Ṣadr School, which still stands in the bazaar of Isfahan. In the hands of these masters he soon became himself an authority in the Islamic sciences and reached a stage in which he even surpassed his teachers.

A few words must be said about the masters with whom Mullā Ṣadrā studied.[3] Mīr Dāmād, his foremost mentor in the "intellectual sciences", was the founder of the philosophical and theosophical school in which Mullā Ṣadrā was trained, the school that is now rapidly becoming known as the "School of Isfahan". A great religious scholar, he was at the same time a logician, mystic and poet. While he taught the Peripatetic doctrines of Ibn Sīnā, he gave them an illuminationist color and himself wrote fine poetry under the pen-name of *ishrāq.* He expounded a rigorously logical philosophy and yet wrote a treatise on a mystical vision he had received in Qum.[4] He harmonised Avicennan cosmology with Shī'ite imamology and made the "fourteen pure ones" (*chahārdah ma'ṣūm*) of Shī'ism the ontological principles of cosmic existence. His own writings dealt mostly with the question of time and creation, in which he expounded the novel view of *ḥudūth-i dahrī* ("eternal creation").[5] His masterpiece, the *Qabasāt* (*Firebrands*), as well as some of his other well-known works such as *Jadhawāt* (*Burning Billets*), which he wrote in Persian, are known in their lithographed editions printed during the last century. But none has received the critical study that this profound but abstruse figure deserves.[6]

The difficulty of Mīr Dāmād's writings has become proverbial, in direct contrast to the lucid and clear writings of his student, Mullā Ṣadrā. It is said in fact that before going on one of his journeys, Mīr Dāmād asked his students to write a treatise in his absence. When he returned and read what Mullā Ṣadrā had written he wept, saying that he was both joyous to have such a student and sad in that he knew that Mullā Ṣadrā's writings would some day overshadow and replace his own. This was in fact a correct prediction. Soon, the clear expositions of the student nearly completely replaced those of the master to whom he owed so much. But Mullā Ṣadrā himself remained completely devoted to his teacher and in several letters addressed to him openly confessed his profound debt to Mīr Dāmād. In fact he preserved his attitude of humility toward Mīr Dāmād even after he had ceased to be in any way in need of him.[7]

Shaykh Bahā' al-Dīn 'Āmilī, the close friend and associate of Mīr Dāmād, was equally celebrated. He was at once theologian, jurisprudent, mathematician, architect, philosopher, occultist and poet. He displayed the versatility usually associated in the Occident with a Renaissance figure and also the profound faith and grounding in religious tradition characteristic of the medieval West. If we were to compare him with Occidental intellectual figures, he would have to be considered as a Leonardo and a St. Anselm or St. Bernard combined into a single person. His versatile genius produced outstanding mathematical treatises, buildings and gardens, irrigation charts that are still in use, theological and juridical treatises which are still studied, and well-known Sufi works. Although he was from the Jabal 'Āmil in the Lebanon and did not learn Persian until the age of twelve,[8] he produced perhaps the finest Persian poetry of the tenth/sixteenth century.

Mullā Ṣadrā studied avidly with Shaykh-i Bahā'ī, as he is usually known in Persia, but almost exclusively in the religious sciences. For the "intellectual sciences" he was more attracted to the circle of Mīr Dāmād. Yet he must certainly have been deeply influenced by Shaykh-i Bahā'ī and his personality, since Ṣadr al-Dīn was a very perceptive student and the character of the teacher was very dominant.

As for Mīr Findiriskī, this enigmatic and yet fascinating figure of Shāh 'Abbās's Ispahan, his associations with Mullā Ṣadrā remain uncertain. Only further research will determine whether Mullā Ṣadrā actually studied with him or not. Mīr Findiriskī, also a close associate of Mīr Dāmād and Shaykh-i Bahā'ī, became famous in later history as a Sufi. He travelled extensively in India, composed two works on the *Yoga Vasiṣṭha,* yet to be edited and studied in detail, wrote a beautiful *qaṣīdah* which summarizes the principles of gnosis, and is credited in popular legend with many miracles. He taught, however, the *Canon* and the *Shifā'* of Ibn Sīnā in Isfahan and the few treatises of his that have survived remain faithful to Peripatetic teachings and negate the ideas which are specifically associated with Mullā Ṣadrā, such as the independent existence of the "world of imagination" and "transsubstantial motion".[9] It is possible that Mīr Findiriskī taught Peripatetic philosophy while he lived the life of a Sufi. In any case, his *qaṣīdah* and the recently discovered treatise on alchemy, not to speak of the works on Hinduism, suffice to confirm the presence of an esoteric side in him and the claim made that he was an outstanding Sufi. Whether, as has been claimed by some, Mullā Ṣadrā learned some of his characteristic ideas from him, rather than from Mīr Dāmād and Shaykh-i Bahā'ī, cannot be substantiated from the existing treatises of Mīr Findiriskī. But since there exist in Islam distinct intellectual perspectives and that there have been figures like Fārābī and Naṣīr al-Dīn Ṭūsī who have been able to place themselves in each perspective and produce authoritative works in them, such a possibility cannot be overlooked in the case of Mīr Findiriskī. It is possible for Mīr Findiriskī to have taught and written Peripatetic works, which are "exoteric" from an intellectual point of view, and also to have transmitted an esoteric teaching to an elite group of his students and disciples. Such examples can be seen elsewhere in the Islamic world and can still be observed in Persia today.

Be that as it may, Mullā Ṣadrā studied avidly in Isfahan with these masters and also associated with the many other students who were then receiving training in Isfahan, some of whom, like

Sayyid Aḥmad 'Alawī, Āqā Ḥusayn Khwānsārī and Mullā Muḥammad Bāqir Sabziwārī, became in turn well-known masters. Mullā Ṣadrā soon became the foremost among them and would have become a celebrated figure even had he chosen to remain in Isfahan. But he sought yet another dimension in the full development of his intellect and personality and so left Isfahan to devote himself to a life of asceticism and inner purification. He thus ended the first period of his life, which was that of formal learning, to begin the second, which was devoted to the spiritual training that Mullā Ṣadrā considered the absolutely essential condition for those who aspire to reach the Divine Mysteries and to gain a true knowledge of *ḥikmat-i ilāhī* or "Divine Science" (literally *theo-sophia*).

The decision of Mullā Ṣadrā to retire from the cosmopolitan center of Isfahan to Kahak, a small and faraway village near Qum, must have been caused by an inner urge to go into solitude; for in solitude are satisfied the needs of the contemplative soul for a direct encounter with the spiritual world in that "inner stillness" which is the prerequisite of all spiritual life. Mullā Ṣadrā must also have needed to evade the outward pressures that he was undergoing at that time. Because he wrote in a simple style and expounded gnostic and metaphysical doctrines openly, he was soon exposed to the attacks of the exoteric *'ulamā'*, some of whom even accused him of infidelity although he was the most pious of men, having never neglected his religious duties throughout his life. The introduction of the *Asfār,* his letters to Mīr Dāmād and the *Sih aṣl* contain in eloquent words his complaint that some of his contemporaries did not understand him. In the introduction of the *Asfār,* he mentions how he was able to master the wisdom of the ancients and the gnostic and theosophical doctrines of the *ḥakīms* before him, and how he had tried in vain to awaken those of his contemporaries who remained ignorant of true knowledge. He continues, "The stifling of the intelligence and congealment of nature, which follow from the hostility of our period, forced me to retire to a faraway place, hiding myself in obscurity and distress, deprived of my hopes and with a broken heart. . . . Putting into practice the instructions of him who is my master and sustainer, the First Imam, ancestor of the holy Imams, the friends and witnesses of God, I started to practice the discipline of dissimulation [*taqiyyah*]".[10] Likewise in his *Sih aṣl,* which is more than any other of his works an autobiographical statement, he attacks the purely exoteric scholars who deny the reality of gnosis and the esoteric dimension of religion. He says, "Some of those who appear to be learned but who are full of evil and corruption, some of the *mutakallimūn* [theologians] who are deprived of correct logic and stand outside the circle of rectitude and the path of salvation, those who follow the religious law yet are deprived of the law of servitude to the Divine and have deviated from the path of belief in metaphysics and eschatology, having tied the rope of blind imitation [*taqlīd*] around their neck, have made the denial of the *dervishes* their slogan."[11]

It would, however, be false to conclude that Mullā Ṣadrā's retreat to Kahak was only for negative reasons. As we shall have the occasion to mention later, he was also urged inwardly to seek a retreat from the turmoils of social life in order to accomplish that inner purification which was the necessary basis for the attainment of the wisdom for which the whole body of his teachings stands. The town of Kahak itself was probably not chosen by accident. It is a small village near Qum off the road between Qum and Isfahan. It sits like a jewel in a valley surrounded by outwardly barren hills with higher mountain chains extending into the horizon. It belongs to that sacred natural *locus* where Qum itself is built, a city which remains to this day a holy center of Persia, prophesied to remain uncorrupted to the end of time, the city where Mullā Ṣadrā's own teacher Mīr Dāmād had received his supreme spiritual vision.

There stands in Kahak today a pentagonal mosque of great beauty going back to the eleventh/seventeenth century, one that is most unusual for a small village. Perhaps Ṣadr al-Dīn lived near this mosque or perhaps it was even built for him. There also stands overlooking the town of one of the hills an *imām-zādah,* the tomb of a saint, of the same period, perhaps the spiritual master who attracted Mullā Ṣadrā to this idyllic and secluded oasis. There are mysterious aspects of his life which have not as yet been unravelled. It is in fact quite possible, as 'Allāmah Ṭabāṭabā'ī believes, that he was initiated into Sufism by Shaykh Bahā' al-Dīn 'Āmilī himself, but his exact spiritual affiliation is still an unsolved problem.

In Islam, spiritual guidance is in general available only through the Sufi orders and the initiation made possible through the regular initiatic chain (*silsilah*) connecting these orders to the origin of the Tradition.[12] In addition, there is the rare instance of those who are initiated by the "invisible hierarchy" or Khaḍir (Khiḍr in Persian) and who are called *afrād*. In Shī'ism there is in addition the possibility of initiation by the Hidden Imam, who is for the Shī'ites the ever-present spiritual pole of the Universe. Certain of the Shī'ite sages like Mīr Dāmād, the gnostic character of whose doctrines can hardly be disputed, did not have a human master, and must be considered as belonging to the second and third categories mentioned above. Others like Sayyid Ḥaydar Āmulī definitely had a human Sufi master. It is hard to decide the situation of Mullā Ṣadrā, to determine definitely whether he received regular Sufi initiation or was inspired by the invisible spiritual hierarchy.[13] Be that as it may, it was during this period of stay in Kahak that Mullā Ṣadrā received his spiritual vision through the spiritual discipline of invocation (*dhikr*) and meditation (*fikr*). During a period that some sources have written to be seven, other eleven and yet others fifteen years, he devoted himself to meditation and spiritual exercise and emerged from this travail as an illuminated sage for whom metaphysics had turned from intellectual understanding to direct vision.

Inasmuch as a great spiritual presence cannot remain ignored for long, Mullā Ṣadrā was soon induced by social pressure to return to public life. Shāh 'Abbās II asked Mullā Ṣadrā to return to his teaching duties and Allāhwirdī Khān built a mosque school, completed by his son, in Shiraz to which Mullā Ṣadrā was invited to teach. Complying with the wishes of the Shah, Ṣadr al-Dīn returned to his native city to begin the last phase of his life, during which he wrote most of his works and trained many students. His personality and science were such that they attracted students from near and far and made Shiraz a great center of learning once again. The Khan school[14] became so famous that it even attracted the attention of foreign travellers. Thomas Herbert, an eleventh/seventeenth century traveller to Persia who visited Shiraz during the lifetime of Mullā Ṣadrā, wrote, "And indeed Shyraz has a Colledge wherein is read Philosophy, Astrology, Physick, Chemistry and the Mathematicks; so as 'tis the more famoused through Persia."[15] Even today the room in which the master taught stands as it must have been when it was the scene of Mullā Ṣadrā's discourse on *ḥikmat* three centuries ago, and the Khan school, despite the dilapidation of some of its parts, remains one of the most beautiful and architecturally perhaps the most important

Safavid building of Shiraz. The school has now been turned over to the Iranian Academy of Philosophy and will undergo major repairs before becoming once again a viable center for the teaching of traditional philosophy.

During this period, which may have lasted up to thirty years, Mullā Ṣadrā, in addition to teaching and writing, made several pilgrimages on foot to Meccā. His intense piety not only continued undiminished but became even more illuminated through the spiritual vision that resulted from years of spiritual practice. It was upon returning from the seventh journey to Mecca that he fell ill and died in Basra in 1050/1640. His tomb was known in that city until a few years ago.[16]

From this brief sketch we can summarize the life of Mullā Ṣadrā by dividing it into three periods:

1. The period of formal education and training in Shiraz and Isfahan.
2. The period of asceticism and self-purification in Kahak, during which he devoted himself almost entirely to the spiritual life but composed a few works including the first part of the *Asfār*, *Ṭarḥ al-kawnayn* (or *Risālat al-ḥashr*), *Ḥudūth al-'ālam* and possibly *Ḥall al-mushkilāt al-falakiyyah fi'l-irādat al-jazāfiyyah*.
3. The period of return to public life in Shiraz, devoted to writing and teaching, during which he wrote all the rest of his works and trained all of his famous students such as Mullā Muḥsin Fayḍ Kāshānī and 'Abd al-Razzāq Lāhījī.

The life of Mullā Ṣadrā is therefore itself an application of his metaphysical doctrines as from another point of view his metaphysical vision was the result of such a life. A life composed of two earlier periods of formal mental training and of inner purification produced its fruit in a third period in which the acute intellectual discipline of the first period and the mystical vision of the second became combined. Nearly all of Mullā Ṣadrā's works, belonging to this third period, are based on these two foundations. Mullā Ṣadrā is in fact the supreme example of that class of sages who combine intellectual discipline with spiritual experience and whom Suhrawardī had called the *muta'allih*.[17] It is in fact for this reason that Mullā Ṣadrā was given the highest title possible within the tradition of *ḥikmat*, the title of *Ṣadr al-muta'allihīn*, meaning foremost amongst the *muta'allihīn* or that group of men who are themselves the elite among all who seek the knowledge of things divine.

* * *

Works

All of the writings of Mullā Ṣadrā are of both intellectual and literary merit. Except for the beautifully written *Sih aṣl,* the poems and a couple of recently discovered treatises which are in Persian, his works are all written in a lucid, simple and flowing Arabic that is among the best examples of philosophical Arabic in the long tradition of Islamic philosophy. Some have divided Mullā Ṣadrā's works into two classes: those devoted to the religious sciences (*naqlī*) and those which concern the intellectual sciences (*'aqlī*). But since Mullā Ṣadrā considered both of these types of sciences to be intimately related, and derived from the single source of knowledge, the luminous Divine Intellect, he has dealt extensively with religious problems in his theosophical works and vice versa. Therefore, such a division is really untenable, although not by any means without meaning.[18]

Nor can his writings be classified chronologically, at least not in the present stage of research. The treatises mentioned above are known to have been written during the middle period of his life. But it is difficult to date the others. Perhaps the major difficulty is in the nature of the works themselves, in that Mullā Ṣadrā, like Suhrawardī, referred back to his works constantly, making additions and changes so that often they appear to have been written almost simultaneously.[19]

The writings of Mullā Ṣadrā range from the monumental *Asfār* to treatises of a few pages. Because of their immense importance most of them were printed in lithographed editions nearly a century ago in Tehran; some have appeared in new editions during the revival of interest in Ṣadr al-Dīn during the past decade, but most still remain to be critically edited and printed in editions that would make the contents of these works more easily accessible.

The bibliographical research of 'Allāmah Ṭabāṭabā'ī, Shaykh Āl-i Muẓaffar, M.T. Danechepazhuh, Sayyid Jalāl al-Dīn Āshtiyānī, H. Corbin and the present author has made more or less known the list of Mullā Ṣadrā's works.[20] But some of the dubious writings need to be further examined and there are still many libraries in both Persia and the subcontinent that need to be catalogued before a definitive bibliography of his writings can be made available.

Basing ourselves on our present-day knowledge of Mullā Ṣadrā's writings, we can enumerate them as follows:

1. *Ajwibat al-masā'il* (*Answers to some Questions*). A recently discovered series of answers to various metaphysical and philosophical questions from the library of the late Mīrzā Ṭahīr Tūnikābunī. The first edition of the text has been printed by S.J. Āshtiyānī in his *Three Treatises* (*Rasā'il-i falsafī*) by Ṣadr al-Dīn Shīrāzī, with English preface by S.H. Nasr, Meshed 1392/1973; pp. 126–98.

2. *Ajwibat al-masā'il al-naṣīriyyah* (*Answers to the Nasirean Questions*) (A.4; C.3; D.P.4).[21] Answers to questions that had been posed by Naṣīr al-Dīn Ṭūsī to Shams al-Dīn 'Abd al-Ḥamīd ibn 'Īsā Khusrawshāhī but which had remained unanswered. These answers have been printed on the margin of Mullā Ṣadrā's *al-Mabda' wa'l-ma'ād*, Tehran, 1314 (A.H. lunar) and of his *Sharḥ al-hidāyah*, Tehran, 1313 (A.H. lunar).

3. *Ajwibah masā'il Shams al-Dīn Muḥammad Gīlānī* (*Answers to the Questions of Shams al-Dīn Gīlānī*) (A.3; C.1). Answers to questions posed by Mullā Shamsā, whom Mullā Ṣadrā addresses in familiar terms. Printed on the margin of *al-Mabda' wa'l-ma'ād*.

4. *Asrār al-āyāt wa anwār al-bayyināt* (*Secrets of the Verses of the Quran and Lights of Evident Truths*) (A.5; C.4; D.P.5). One of Mullā Ṣadrā's main gnostic commentaries upon the Quran, consisting of an introduction and ten chapters. Printed with the commentary of Mullā 'Alī Nūrī, Tehran, 1319 (A.H. lunar).

5. *Dībācha-yi 'arsh al-taqdīs* (*Introduction to "The Throne of Divinity"*) (A.18; C.5; D.P.18). An introduction in Arabic – despite its Persian title – to Mīr Dāmād's *'Arsh al-taqdīs*, in which he praises highly Mīr Dāmād.

6. *Dīwān* (*Diwan*) (A.19; C.6; D.P.19). Poems collected by his student Mullā Muḥsin Fayḍ, but not of the same quality as the poems of Fayḍ himself. Some of them have been published by S.H. Nasr as an appendix to his edition of *Sih aṣl*.

7. *al-Ḥashr (Risālah fī* (*Treatise on Resurrection*) (A.14; C.8; D.P.14). Also known as *Ṭarḥ al-kawnayn fī ḥashr al-ālamayn*, it deals in eight chapters with the resurrection and

return of all things to God, including the mineral kingdom. Printed on the margin of *al-Mabda' wa'l-ma'ād*; on the margin of *Kashf al-fawā'id* of al-Ḥillī, 1305 (A.H. lunar); and in Mullā Ṣadrā's *Rasā'il,* Tehran, 1302 (A.H. lunar).

8. *al-Ḥikmat al-'arshiyyah (Kitāb) (The Book of Theosophy descending from the Divine Throne)* (A.15; C.9; D.P.15). One of Mullā Ṣadrā's major works, dealing in two sections with God and eschatology. The work is particularly significant in that it summarizes Mullā Ṣadrā's teachings on eschatology and man's posthumous becoming. This book was a major source of controversy among later schools of theology and was commented upon by Shaykh Aḥmad Aḥsā'ī, the founder of the Shaykhī movement, who criticized it, and by Mullā Ismā'īl Iṣfahānī, who answered these criticisms. It was printed in Tehran, 1315 (A.H. lunar), and again in Isfahan in 1341 (A.H. solar) with a Persian translation by Ghulām Ḥusayn Āhanī.

9. *al-Ḥikmat al-muta'āliyah fi'l-asfār al-'aqliyyat al-arba'ah (The Transcendent Theosophy concerning the Four Intellectual Journeys of the Soul)*, usually known simply as *Asfār* (*Journeys*) (A.16; C.10; D.P.16). Mullā Ṣadrā's *magnum opus,* it will be treated separately in the next chapter. It was lithographed in Tehran, 1282 (A.H. lunar), and a new edition has been edited by 'Allāmah Sayyid Muḥammad Ḥusayn Ṭabāṭabā'ī, which has appeared over the years since 1378 (A.H. lunar) in Tehran. Thus far nine volumes have appeared containing parts (*asfār*) one, three and four with 'Allāmah Ṭabāṭabā'ī's own commentary in addition to selections from older commentaries. Unfortunately, part two dealing with substances and accidents has not as yet been published in the new edition and there seems to be no plan to include it in this edition. A Persian translation of the *Asfār* has been made by J. Muṣliḥ, vols. I and II including a summary of the first and third *safar* and the fourth *safar* being translated in its entirety. See J. Muṣliḥ, *Falsafa-yi 'ālī yā ḥikmat-i Ṣadr al-muta'allihīn, talkhīṣ wa tarjuma-yi qismat-i umūr-i 'āmmah wa ilāhiyyāt-i kitāb-i asfār,* Tehran 1353 (A.H. solar); and *'Ilm al-nafs yā rawānshināsī-yi safar-i nafs-i kitāb-i asfār,* Tehran, 1352 (A.H. solar).

10. *Ḥudūth al-'ālam (Risālah fī) (Treatise on the Temporal Genesis of the World)* (A.13; C.11; D.P.13). Discusses the genesis of the world in time based on Mullā Ṣadrā's doctrine of transsubstantial motion (*al-ḥarakat al-jawhariyyah*) and rejects the views of Mīr Dāmād. A discussion is given of the views of

the pre-Socratic philosophers. Printed in Mullā Ṣadrā's *Rasā'il*, Tehran, 1302 (A.H. lunar).

11. *Iksīr al-'ārifīn fī ma'rifah ṭarīq al-ḥaqq wa'l-yaqīn* (*The Elixir of Gnostics concerning the Knowledge of the Path of Truth and Certainty*) (A.6; C.12; D.P.6). In four sections on the classification of the sciences and on the nature of man. Printed in the *Rasā'il*, 1302 (A.H. lunar).

12. *al-Imāmah (Risālah fī)* (*Treatise on the Imamate*) (C.13). Mentioned only by Āqā Buzurg in *al-Dharī'ah* (vol. II, p. 333), no manuscript of this work has as yet been discovered although 'Allāmah Ṭabāṭabā'ī has stated that when he was in Tabriz in his youth he saw a manuscript of it and it contained a treatment of Mullā Ṣadrā's gnostic view of the Imamate.

13. *Ittiḥād al-'āqil wa'l-ma'qūl (Risālah fī)* (*Treatise on the Unity of the Intellect and the Intelligible*) (A.1; C.14; D.P.1). According to *al-Dharī'ah*, vol. I, p. 81, this treatise has been published in Tehran but we have not been able to find the printed version. It includes an exposition of Mullā Ṣadrā's famous doctrin of the union of the Intellect and the intelligible.

14. *Ittiṣāf al-māhiyyah bi'l-wujūd (Risālah fī)* (*Treatise on the Doctrine that Existence is a Predicate of Quiddity*) (A.2; C.15; D.P.2). Discusses the relation between existence and quiddity in a manner that is opposed to his views in the *Mashā'ir*. He also criticizes Fakhr al-Dīn Rāzī and Dawānī. Printed in the *Rasā'il*, Tehran, 1302 (A.H. lunar) and on the margin of his *al-Taṣawwur wa'l-taṣdīq*, lithographed in Tehran, 1311 (A.H. lunar).

15. *Kasr al-aṣnām al-jāhiliyyah fī dhamm al-mutaṣawwifīn* (*Demolition of the Idols of Ignorance in Blaming those who Pretend to Sufism*) (A.27; C.16; D.P.28). The word "*mutaṣawwifīn*" referred to here is not used according to its usual meaning of one who follows Sufism but means one who pretends to follow it. In this treatise, Mullā Ṣadrā criticizes the excesses of those in his day who, pretending to be Sufis, disregarded the *Sharī'ah* and its teachings. Edited in a critical edition by M.T. Danechepazhuh, Tehran, 1340 (A.H. solar).

16. *Khalq al-a'māl (Risālah fī)* (*Treatise on the Creation of Human Actions*) (A.17; C.17; D.P.17). A discussion of free will and determinism in which Mullā Ṣadrā takes into consideration the views of different schools of *kalām* and *falsafah* before stating his own view. Printed in the *Rasā'il*, Tehran, 1302 (A.H.

lunar) and with the *Kashf al-fawā'id* of al-Ḥillī and *Ḥaqā'iq al-īmān* of Shahīd Thānī, Tehran, 1305 (A.H. lunar). This treatise has also been edited and published by M.A. Rawḍātī as *Risāla-yi jabr wa tafwīḍ ma'rūf bi-khalq al-a'māl*, with an introduction by the editor and a short preface by J. Humā'ī, Isfahan, 1340 (A.H. solar).

17. *al-Lama'āt al-mashriqiyyah fi'l-funūn al-manṭiqiyyah* (*Illuminationist Gleamings in the Art of Logic*) (A.10; C.38; D.P.10). Cited by the three earlier bibliographical works as *Tanqiyah*, this is a short but important work on logic, written partly in the style of Suhrawardī's *Ḥikmat al-ishrāq* and containing in nine chapters some of Mullā Ṣadrā's own new contributions to logic. It also mentions some of the metaphysical ideas which are distinctly his own. Printed with a somewhat free Persian translation and long commentary by 'A. Mishkātaddīnī under the title *Manṭiq-i nuwīn* Tehran, (1347 A.H. solar).

18. *Limmiyyah ikhtiṣāṣ al-minṭaqah bi-mawdi' mu'ayyan fi'l-falak (Maqālah fi)* (*Treatise on Why the Zodiac is Located in a Determined Position of the Sphere*) (A.28; C.18; D.P.29). An as yet neglected treatise on this astronomical question.

19. *al-Mabda' wa'l-ma'ād (Kitāb)* (*The Book of the Origin and Return*) (A.29; C.20; D.P.30). One of Mullā Ṣadrā's important works dealing with metaphysics, cosmogony and eschatology. Printed in Tehran, 1314 (A.H. lunar) with the commentary of Ḥājjī Mullā Hādī Sabziwārī. Āshtiyānī has just completed a new critical edition, based upon a manuscript in the handwriting of 'Abd al-Razzāq Lāhījī, Mullā Ṣadrā's student, existing in the library of 'Allāmah Ṭabāṭabā'ī in Qum, under the title *al-Mabda' wa'l-ma'ād* (*The Beginning and the End*), with prolegomena and notes by Āshtiyānī, Persian and English introductions by S.H. Nasr, Tehran, 1976.

20. *Mafātīḥ al-ghayb* (*Keys to the Invisible World*) (A.35; C.21; D.P.36). A basic work of Mullā Ṣadrā's period of maturity combining gnostic doctrines on metaphysics, cosmology and eschatology and containing ample references to the Quran and *Ḥadīth*. It has been among the most frequently studied of Mullā Ṣadrā's works and was lithographed in Tehran, n.d., and again along with the *Sharḥ uṣūl al-kāfī* with Sabziwārī's commentary, Tehran, 1282 (A.H. lunar); reprinted, Tehran, 1391 (A.H. lunar). A partial Persian translation, made during the Qajar period and including the introduction and part of the first chapter of the book, has been published by M. Mohaghegh in

Maqālāt wa barrasīhā (Dānishkada-yi ilāhiyyāt wa ma'ārif-i islāmī, Tehran), vol. 2, Summer, 1349 (A.H. solar), pp. 56–79.

21. *al-Masā'il al-qudsiyyah fi'l-ḥikmat al-muta'āliyah* (*Spiritual Questions concerning the Transcendent Theosophy*). This work of Mullā Ṣadrā, recently discovered in the Majlis Library of Tehran,[22] must be one of his last works, written as it was in 1049/1639, a year before he died. It includes in three chapters of mixed Arabic and Persian a discussion of ontology and proof for the existence of the "imaginal world", the archetypes and "mental existence". Mullā Ṣadrā mentions in this work, as in the *Mashā'ir,* that he first followed the view of principiality of quiddity and only later accepted the principiality of being. This work is contained in S.J. Āshtiyānī, *Three Treatises* (second treatise).

22. *al-Mashā'ir (Kitāb)* (*The Book of Metaphysical Penetrations*) (A.30; C.22; D.P.33). One of Mullā Ṣadrā's cardinal works and his most studied *opus* in recent years, containing the synopsis of his ontology. This work was thoroughly studied by later Persian *ḥakīms* and subjected to many commentaries including those of Shaykh Aḥmad Aḥsā'ī, Mullā 'Alī Nūrī, Mullā Muḥammad Ja'far Langarūdī Lāhījī, Mullā Ismā'īl Iṣfahānī, Mīrzā Aḥmad Ardakānī Shīrāzī, Mullā Zayn al-'Ābidīn ibn Muḥammad Ja'far Nūrī and Mīrzā Ḥasan Jilwah.[23] After being lithographed in Tehran, 1315 (A.H. lunar), it was published in a critical edition by Corbin with the Persian translation of the Qajar prince-philosopher Badī' al-Mulk Mīrzā 'Imād al-Dawlah and a French translation which is the first of a complete work of Mullā Ṣadrā into a European language. A new Persian translation by Ghulām Ḥusayn Āhanī appeared in Isfahan, 1340 (A.H. solar), while the commentary of Langarūdī was published in a critical edition by S.J. Āshtiyānī with extensive introductions by himself and J. Humā'ī and an English preface by S.H. Nasr, Meshed, 1381 (A.H. lunar). It is now being translated into Japanese by T. Izutsu.

23. *al-Maẓāhir al-ilāhiyyah fī asrār al-'ulūm al-kamāliyyah* (*Book of Divine Theophanies concerning the Secrets of the Sciences that Lead to Perfection*) (A.33; C.23; D.P.34). Deals in six sections with a series of metaphysical questions which are studied with reference to Quranic citations. Lithographed on the margin of *al-Mabda' wa'l-ma'ād,* it was given a new edition by S.J. Āshtiyānī, Meshed, 1381 (A.H. lunar).

24. *al-Mizāj (Risālah fī)* (*Treatise on Temperament*) (A.32;

C.24; D.P.31). Discusses Mullā Ṣadrā's own views on temperament as a branch of the "science of the soul", summarizing his thought as contained in the *Asfār* in the section on substances and accidents.

25. *Mutashābihāt al-qur'ān* (*On the Metaphorical Verses of the Quran*) (A.31; C.25; D.P.31). An early work of Mullā Ṣadrā, dealing in a gnostic manner with the difficult verses of the Holy Quran and including material that is also treated in his commentary upon the *āyat al-kursī* and in the *Mafātīḥ al-ghayb*. This work is contained in S.J. Āshtiyānī, *Three Treatises* (first treatise).

26. *Nāma-yi Ṣadrā bi ustād-i khud Sayyid Mīr Dāmād* (I) (*The Letter of Ṣadr al-Dīn to his Teacher Mīr Dāmād*). An Arabic letter, whose incomplete text has been published by Āshtiyānī in his *Sharḥ-i ḥāl wa ārā'-i falsafī-yi Mullā Ṣadrā*, Meshed, 1381 (A.H. lunar), pp. 225–28, and also by M. Walā'ī, "Ṣadr al-muta'allihīn", *Nāma-yi āstāna-yi quds,* vol. I, no. 9, Ādhar 1340, pp. 56–62.

Beginning:

هذه صورة مكتوب الذى كتب صدر الحكماء...

End:

كما يجوزون ان يكون بعض اجناس الجواهر من بعض آخر و يقولون جواهر العالم.

27. *Nāma-yi Ṣadrā bi ustād-i khud Sayyid Mīr Dāmād* (II) (Persian). Second of four letters known to have been written by Mullā Ṣadrā to Mīr Dāmād.

Beginning:

قسم بمبدعى واجب الوجود

End:

در مكتب او كرد همين خوانده فراموش صورت كتابت به اختتام رسيد

Published by M.T. Danechepazhuh, *Rāhnamā-yi kitāb*, vol. V, no. 8–9, 1341 (A.H. solar), pp. 757–65.

28. *Nâma-yi Ṣadrā bi ustâd-i khud Sayyid Mīr Dāmād* (III) (Persian and Arabic). Third of four known letters of Mullā Ṣadrâ to Mīr Dâmâd.

Beginning:

لا زال شموس الحكمة الايمانية

End:

بحقّ محمّد و آله الاطهار صلوات الله العزيز الجبار

Published by M.T. Danechepazhuh, *Farhang-i īrān zamīn*, vol. 13, no. 1–4, 1966, pp. 84–95.

29. *Nâma-yi Ṣadrā bi ustâd-i khud Sayyid Mīr Dâmâd* (IV) (Persian). Fourth of Mullā Ṣadrâ's known letters to Mīr Dâmâd.

Beginning:

كفى شرفاً انى مضاف اليكم

End:

مشاراليه را كلمه‌اى چند....

The incomplete text, published by M.T. Danechepazhuh in *Farhang-i īrān zamīn*, vol. 13, no. 1–4, 1966, pp. 95–98, ends abruptly with the words cited above. The British Museum MS. Or. 2852 contains the complete text of this letter but it has not yet been published.

30. *al-Qaḍā' wa'l-qadar fī af'āl al-bashar (Risālah fī mas'alah)* (*Treatise on the Problem of Divine Decree and Destiny concerning the Actions of Man*) (A.26; C.28; D.P.27). Deals with predestination and free will and how divine providence can include what appears to man as evil. Published in the *Rasā'il*, Tehran, 1302 (A.H. lunar).

31. *al-Qudsiyyah fī asrār al-nuqṭat al-ḥissiyyat al-mushīrah ilā asrār al-huwiyyah (al-Risālah)* (*The Sacred Treatise on the Mysteries of the Sensible Point which Alludes to the Mysteries of Divine Identity*) (A.20; C.29; D.P.20). On the "science of letters" and the esoteric significance of the point. Its authenticity is doubted by Āshtiyânī. Lithographed on the margin of *al-Mabda' wa'l-ma'ād*, Tehran, 1314 (A.H. lunar).

32. *Risāla-yi fârsī mansūb bi-Mullā Ṣadrā* (*Persian Treatise attributed to Mullā Ṣadrā*). A recently discovered work of Ṣadr

al-Dīn in Persian, from a collection belonging to the library of Dr. Asadallāh Khāwarī in Shiraz containing fourteen treatises (pp. 144–8 of this collection). The treatise was discovered by Mr. K. Ra'nā Ḥusaynī and is written in lucid Persian. It contains ideas which are certainly those of Mullā Ṣadrā, so that there is no reason to doubt its authenticity.[24]

33. *Sarayān nūr wujūd al-ḥaqq fi'l-mawjūdāt* (*The Penetration of the Light of the Divine Truth in Creatures*) (A.21; C.30; D.P.21). A work of his youth, when Mullā Ṣadrā still believed in the principiality of quiddity rather than of being. Some have attributed this work to Mullā Muḥsin Fayḍ Kāshānī. Lithographed as part of the *Rasā'il*, Tehran, 1302 (A.H. lunar).

34. *Sharḥ al-hidāyat al-athīriyyah* (*Commentary upon the "Book of Guidance" of Athīr al-Dīn Abharī*) (A.24; C.32; D.P.24). A masterly commentary upon the famous *Kitāb al-hidāyah* of Abharī in which Mullā Ṣadrā expounds a cycle of Peripatetic philosophy without dealing with his own particular doctrines. This work, which also displays his knowledge of mathematics, received much attention in Persia and many glosses were written upon it, such as those of Mullā 'Alī Zunūzī and Mīrzā Abu'l-Ḥasan Jilwah. It also became particularly famous in the Indo-Pakistani subcontinent. A very large number of glosses and commentaries have been written upon it.[25] Both S.J. Āshtiyānī and 'A. Zaryāb Khu'ī are preparing new editions of the work.

35. *Sharḥ Uṣūl al-kāfī* (*Commentary upon the Uṣūl al-kāfī*) (A.23; C.33; D.P.23). Perhaps the most important commentary ever written on this basic source book of Shī'ism, it is one of Mullā Ṣadrā's main religious works and deals in a gnostic manner with most of the basic themes of Shī'ism. Although a large work as it stands, it was never completed, for the commentary on the text reached only up to Chapter XI of the *Kitāb al-ḥujjah*. Its abrupt break in the middle of a vast doctrinal development has been compared, not without justice, to the sudden interruption of Bach's *Art of the Fugue*.[26] Lithographed along with the *Mafātīḥ al-ghayb*, Tehran, 1282 (A.H. lunar); reprinted, Tehran, 1391 (A.H. lunar); and lithographed independently, Tehran, n.d.

36. *al-Shawāhid al-rubūbiyyah fi'l-manāhij al-sulūkiyyah* (*Divine Witnesses concerning the Paths of Spiritual Realization*) (A.25; C.34; D.P.26). Mullā Ṣadrā's "personal" masterpiece, which in five chapters written from a gnostic point of view

summarizes more than any other work his own doctrines. It is one of his works most frequently commented upon, having been commented upon by such later masters as Mullā 'Alī Nūrī, Āqā Muḥammad Riḍā Qumsha'ī and Sabziwārī. The monumental commentary of Sabziwārī, a masterpiece in itself, has been published along with the text of the *Shawāhid* in a critical edition by S.J. Āshtiyānī. It includes an extensive introduction by the editor and an English introduction by S.H. Nasr, Meshed, 1346 (A.H. solar). The lithographed edition of Tehran, 1281 (A.H. lunar) also contains Sabziwārī's commentary but in a form less complete than that given by Āshtiyānī.

37. *Sih aṣl (Risāla-yi)* (*Treatise on the Three Principles*) (A.22; C.31; D.P.22). Mullā Ṣadrā's most important Persian work, containing an autobiographical defense of his position and a treatment of the "science of the soul" in the light of the "Transcendent Theosophy". A critical edition of this work has been published along with an introduction concerning the author and this work by S.H. Nasr, Tehran, 1340 (A.H. solar).

38. *al-Tafsīr* (*Commentary upon the Quran*) (A.9; C.35; D.P.9). Containing commentaries upon the following sections: *al-Fātiḥah*; Surah 2 (*al-Baqarah*) up to verse 61 and also *āyat al-kursī* (v. 256); *āyat al-nūr* (v. 35) in Surah 24 (*al-Nūr*); Surah 27 (*al-Naml*), v. 88.; Surah 32 (*al-Sajdah*); Surah 36 (*Yā-sīn*); Surah 56 (*al-Wāqi'ah*); Surah 57 (*al-Ḥadīd*); Surah 62 (*al-Jumu'ah*); Surah 65 (*al-Ṭalāq*); Surah 86 (*al-Ṭāriq*); Surah 87 (*al-A'lā*); Surah 93 (*al-Ḍuḥā*); Surah 99 (*al-Zilzāl*). This work is an important example of the hermeneutic and esoteric commentary upon the Quran of which Mullā Ṣadrā was a master. Lithographed with the glosses of Mullā 'Alī Nūrī, Tehran, 1321 and 1322 (A.H. lunar). The commentary upon *āyat al-nūr* was also lithographed separately, Tehran, 1313 (A.H. lunar).

39. *Tafsīr al-ḥadīth*

الناس نيام فاذا ماتوا انتبهوا

(*Commentary upon the ḥadīth, "Man is asleep and when he dies he awakens".*) A gnostic interpretation of this prophetic saying, cited by 'Allāmah Ṭabāṭabā'ī.[27] The commentary upon this *ḥadīth* has also been given by Mullā Ṣadrā in his commentary upon the Quran, in the chapter on surah *Yā sīn.*[28]

40. *Ta'līqāt 'alā ilāhiyyāt kitāb al-shifā'* (*Glosses upon the Metaphysics of the "Book of Remedy" of Ibn Sīnā*) (A.14;

C.36; D.P.12). Masterly glosses upon the *Shifā'* up to *maqālah* six of the metaphysics, expounding Ibn Sīnā's views with occasional reference to his own. Lithographed on the margin of the *Shifā'*, Tehran, 1303 (A.H. lunar).

41. *Ta'līqāt 'alā sharḥ ḥikmat al-ishrāq* (*Glosses upon the Commentary upon the "Theosophy of the Orient of Light" of Suhrawardī*) (A.11; C.27; D.P.11). A work that is based directly upon the text of Suhrawardī rather than upon Quṭb al-Dīn Shīrāzī's commentary, it is a fundamental study of *ishrāqī* theosophy and its comparison with the *mashshā'ī* school. Corbin has prepared a translation which has not yet been published[29] and Āshtiyānī has announced a new edition. Lithographed on the margin of *Sharḥ ḥikmat al-ishrāq*, Tehran, 1315 (A.H. lunar).

42. *al-Taṣawwur wa'l-taṣdīq (Risālah fī)* (*Treatise on Concept and Judgment*) (C.39; D.P.8). An analysis and discussion of the logical problems of concept and judgement. Lithographed on the margin of al-Ḥillī's *al-Jawhar al-naḍīd*, Tehran, 1311 (A.H. lunar).

43. *al-Tashakhkhuṣ (Risālah fī)* (*Treatise on Individuation*) (A.7; C.40; D.P.7). An important though short treatise on one of the difficult problems of traditional philosophy. Lithographed in the *Rasā'il*.

44. *al-Wāridāt al-qalbiyyah fī ma'rifat al-rubūbiyyah* (*The Inspirations of the Heart concerning Knowledge of the Divinity*) (A.38; C.41; D.P.39). A criticism of worldly scholars, especially those of his contemporaries who supported oppressive rulers for worldly ends. Printed in the *Rasā'il*, Tehran, 1302 (A.H. lunar). A complete Persian translation with commentary by A. Shafī'īhā (Chafiiha) was published by The Iranian Academy of Philosophy (Tehran, 1358/1978).

45. *al-Wujūd (Risālah)* (*Treatise on Being*) (C.42; D.P.40). A treatise on ontology discovered by M.T. Danechepazhuh.

46. *Zād al-musāfir* (Provisions of the Traveller). A masterly summary of the doctrines pertaining to eschatology made known only recently. Edited by Kāẓim Mudīr Shānachī from a unique manuscript in his own collection, in *Nashriyya-yi Dānishkada-yi Ilāhiyyāt wa Ma'ārif-i Islāmī-i Dānishgāh-i Mashhad*, no. 2, Spring 1351 (A.H. solar), pp. 134–44.

In addition, the following works have been attributed to Mullā Ṣadrā, but their authorship remains uncertain:

1. *Ādāb al-baḥth wa'l-munāẓarah.*
2. *al-Fawā'id (Risālah fī).*
3. *Ithbāt al-bāri' (Risālah fī).*
4. *Jawābāt al-masā'il al-'awīsah* (most likely by Mīr Dāmād).
5. *al-Qawā'id al-malakūtiyyah (Risālah fī)* (most likely the same as *al-Masā'il al-qudsiyyah).*
6. *Sirr al-nuqṭah.*

Finally it must be mentioned that 'Allāmah Ṭabāṭabā'ī told us that in his youth in Tabriz he saw a collection of treatises of Mullā Ṣadrā on *Arwāḥ*, the *Barzakh* and *Qaḍā' wa'l-qadar* different from the well-known treatise of this name. This collection, however, has not as yet been located.

Undoubtedly further research in libraries, especially in those of Persia, Afghanistan, Pakistan and India, will bring to light new works of Mullā Ṣadrā as well as new manuscripts of presently known writings. Meanwhile the recognized works, a list of which has been given above, must be edited and studied to make better known the monumental metaphysical edifice which was erected by the sage of Shiraz and to make possible the establishment of the relation of these works to each other in both a chronological and a doctrinal manner.

Notes

1. For the traditional account of the life of Mullā Ṣadrā see *Rawḍāt al-jannāt* of Muḥammad Khwānsārī, vol. II, Tehran, 1306 (A.H. lunar), pp. 331–2; *Rawḍat al-ṣafā'*, the appendices (*Mulḥaqāt*) of Riḍā Qulī Khān Hidāyat, vol. VIII, Tehran, 1270 (A.H. lunar), p. 129; *Mustadrak al-wasā'il* of Ḥājj Mīrzā Ḥusayn Nūrī, vol. III, Tehran, 1321 (A.H. lunar), pp. 422–3; *Amal al-āmil* of Muḥammad ibn al-Ḥasan al-Ḥurr al-'Āmilī, Tehran, 1302 (lunar), p. 58 (note by Muḥammad Qummī); *Salāfat al-'aṣr fī maḥāsin al-shu'arā' bi kull miṣr* of Sayyid 'Alī Ṣadr al-Dīn al-Madanī, Cairo, 1324 (A.H. lunar), p. 499; *Rayḥānat al-adab* of Muḥammad 'Alī Tabrīzī, vol. II, Tehran, 1331 (A.H. solar), pp. 458–61; *Qiṣaṣ al-'ulamā'* of Mīrzā Muḥammad Tunikābunī, Tehran, 1313 (A.H. solar), pp. 329–33.
As for modern studies devoted to his life in Muslim languages see Abū 'Abdallāh Zanjānī, *al-Faylasūf al-fārsī al-kabīr Ṣadr al-Dīn al-Shīrāzī*, Damascus, 1936; Muḥmūd Muḥammad al-Khuḍayrī, "Ṣadr al-Dīn al-Shīrāzī", *Risālat al-islām*, no. 2, 1950, pp. 212–18 and no. 3, 1951, pp. 318–27; Ja'far Āl-i Yāsīn, *Ṣadr al-Dīn al-Shīrāzī, Mujaddid al-falsafat al-islāmiyyah*, Baghdad, 1375 (A.H. lunar); the introduction of Shaykh Muḥammad Riḍā Āl-i Muẓaffar to the new edition of the *Asfār*, vol. I, Qum, 1378 (A.H. lunar); Abū Maḥfūẓ al-Karīm Ma'ṣūmī, "Ṣadr al-Dīn al-Shīrāzī", Indo-Iranica, vol. XIV, no. 4, December 1961, pp. 27–42 (of Persian-Arabic section); Sayyid Jalāl al-Dīn Āshtiyānī,

Sharḥ-i ḥàl wa àrà'-i falsafi-yi Mullà Ṣadrà, Meshed, 1381 (A.H. lunar); S.H. Nasr (ed.), *Mullà Ṣadrà Commemoration Volume*, Tehran, 1380/1961; and the introduction of S.H. Nasr to his edition of Mullà Ṣadrà's *Sih aṣl*, Tehran, 1380/1961.

Works in European languages dealing with Mullà Ṣadrà's life include H. Corbin's introduction (Chapter I) to his translation of Mullà Ṣadrà's *Kitàb al-mashà'ir* under the title *Le livre des pénétrations métaphysiques*, Tehran-Paris, 1964; Comte de Gobineau, *Les religions et les philosophies dans l'Asie Centrale*, pp. 79–88; E.G. Browne, *A Literary History of Persia*, vol. IV, 1969, pp. 429–30; Browne, *A Year Among the Persians*, London, (published originally in 1893), 1950, pp. 141–3; S.H. Nasr, *Islamic Studies*, Chapter 10, "Ṣadr al-Dìn Shìràzì (Mullà Ṣadrà), His Life, Doctrines and Significance"; and Nasr, "Mullà Ṣadrà" in *Encyclopedia of Philosophy*.

2. See Nasr, introduction to *Sih aṣl*, p. 2; Corbin, *Le livre des pénétrations métaphysiques*, p. 2. See also the introduction to Sayyid Muḥammad Mishkàt to *Maḥajjat al-bayḍà'* of Fayḍ Kàshànì, vol. I, Tehran, 1380 (A.H. lunar), pp. 13–24.
3. See note 9 of chapter I for sources on Mìr Dàmàd; as for Shaykh Bahà' al-Dìn Àmilì and Mìr Findiriskì, see Nasr, "The School of Ispahan" and the chapter to appear shortly in vol. VI of the *Cambridge History of Iran*; S.H. Nasr, "Mìr Findiriskì", in the *New Encyclopedia of Islam*.
4. See Corbin, "Confessions extatiques de Mìr Dàmàd".
5. See Nasr, "The School of Ispahan", p. 917.
6. As already mentioned, a critical edition of the *Qabasàt* is now being prepared by M. Mohaghegh, and several other collaborators. T. Izutsu is writing an extensive philosophical analysis of this work.
7. The text of the letter of Mullà Ṣadrà to Mìr Dàmàd has been published by Àshtiyànì in his *Sharḥ-i ḥàl wa àrà'*, pp. 225–8. Considering the fact that Mullà Ṣadrà was not in the habit of overpraising people the titles with which he addresses Mìr Dàmàd (p. 225) are indicative of his deep respect for his teacher.
8. The famous Persian scholar Sa'ìd Naficy, the only person to have devoted a separate study to him, calls him the most outstanding poet of his age. See his *Aḥwàl wa ash'àr-i Shaykh-i Bahà'ì*, Tehran, 1316 (A.H. solar).
9. On the writings of Mìr Findiriskì and commentary upon their contrast with the works of Mullà Ṣadrà see H. Corbin and S.J. Àshtiyànì, *Anthologie des philosophes iraniens*, Tehran-Paris, 1972, pp. 63–97 of the Persian and 31–47 of the French text. Also see S.H. Nasr, "Mìr Findiriskì", in the *New Encyclopedia of Islam*.
10. Mullà Ṣadrà, *al-Ḥikmat al-muta'àliyah fi'l-asfàr al-'aqliyyat al-arba'ah*, ed. by M.H. Ṭabàṭabà'ì, vol. I, 1378 (A.H. lunar), p. 8.
11. Mullà Ṣadrà, *Sih aṣl*, pp. 5–6.
12. See F. Schuon, *Understanding Islam*, trans. by D.M. Matheson, London, 1963, Chapter IV; S.H. Nasr, *Ideals and Realities of Islam*, London, 1966, Chapter IV; and M. Lings, *A Sufi Saint of the Twentieth Century*, London, 1971.
13. Corbin is of the view that he definitely did not have a human master. As far as we are concerned, however, the question cannot be determined so categorically.
14. On the Khan School, its historical background, architecture, decorations and testament of endowment (*waqf-nàmah*), see H. Khoubnazar and W. Kleiss, "Die Madrasa-yi Ḫàn in Schiras", *Archaeologische Mitteilungen aus Iran*, vol. 8, 1975, pp. 255–78.
15. Thomas Herbert, *Some Years Travells into Diverse Parts of Africa and Asia the Great*, London, 1677, p. 129.
16. The outstanding contemporary master of the school of Mullà Ṣadrà, Ḥaḍrat-i Àyatallàh Sayyid Abu'l-Ḥasan Rafì'ì Qazwìnì, told us that nearly forty years

ago, one of the Arab *sayyids* of Basra discovered in that city a tomb with the name of Mullā Ṣadrā engraved on the stone. Some years later when friends went to visit it, the tombstone had disappeared. See S.H. Nasr (ed.), *Mullā Ṣadrā Commemoration Volume*, p. 11.

17. See Nasr, *Three Muslim Sages*, p. 64.
18. In our introduction to the *Sih aṣl*, pp. 9–12, we have divided his works in this manner.
19. In his study of the bibliography of Mullā Ṣadrā in the *Mullā Ṣadrā Commemoration Volume*, M.T. Danechepazhuh has stated in many cases the names of other of Mullā Ṣadrā's books which he mentions in the treatises under discussion.
20. The following bibliographical studies of Mullā Ṣadrā may be mentioned: 'Allāmah Ṭabāṭabā'ī, "Ṣadr al-Dīn Muḥammad ibn Ibrāhīm Shīrāzī. . . .", *Mullā Ṣadrā Commemoration Volume*, pp. 107–20; Āshtiyānī, *Sharḥ-i ḥāl wa ārā'*, pp. 210–25, repeated with a few minor changes in his prolegomena to the *Three Treatises* of Mullā Ṣadrā (no. 1 of bibliography); H. Corbin, *Le livre des pénétrations métaphysiques*, pp. 27–41; Abū Maḥfūẓ al-Karīm Ma'ṣūmī, "Ṣadr al-Dīn al-Shīrāzī, ḥayātuhu wa ma'āthiruhu", *Indo-Iranica*, vol. 14, Dec. 1961, pp. 37–40; Nasr, introduction to *Sih aṣl*, pp. 9–12.

    Abū Maḥfūẓ al-Karīm Ma'ṣūmī has given valuable information on manuscripts and commentaries of Mullā Ṣadrā's works in the subcontinent in his article, "Ṣadr al-Dīn al-Shīrāzī".

    See also further studies of M.T. Danechepazhuh in his introduction to Mullā Ṣadrā's *Kasr al-aṣnām al-jāhiliyyah* and in his "Nuktahā'ī dar bāra-yi āthār-i Mullā Ṣadrā", *Rāhnamā-yi kitāb*, vol. V, no. 1, Farvardin 1341 (A.H. solar), pp. 33–40. Also, in his catalogue of the manuscripts of the Tehran University Library (*Fihrist-i kitābkhāna-yi ihdā'ī-yi āqā-yi Sayyid Muḥammad Mishkāt bi kitābkhāna-yi dānishgāh-i Tihrān*, 1332 onward (A.H. solar), Danechepazhuh has provided a wealth of information about the works of Mullā Ṣadrā. His references to Mullā Ṣadrā are scattered throughout the many volumes of this vast work.
21. In this bibliography C. refers to the catalogue of Corbin mentioned in the previous footnote, D.P. to that of Danechepazhuh in the *Mullā Ṣadrā Commemoration Volume* and A. to the work of Āshtiyānī on Mullā Ṣadrā's writings mentioned above.
22. See 'Abd al-Ḥusayn Ḥā'irī, *Fihrist-i kitābkhāna-yi shawrā-yi millī*, vol. IX, part I, 1346 (A.H. solar), p. 389; and part IX, 1347, pp. 948–9.
23. For a thorough discussion of the *Kitāb al-mashā'ir* and commentaries written upon it see Corbin, *Le livre des pénétrations métaphysiques*, chapter III.
24. The treatise, which begins with the words . . .

    اللهمّ اشد عضده

    and ends with the phrase

    سبحان ربک رب العزة عما یصفون و سلام علی المرسلین و الحمدلله رب العالمین

    is published in the *Revue de la Faculté des Lettres et des Sciences Humaines* of Tehran University, vol. 17, no. 3–4, 1349 (A.H. solar), pp. 326–9.
25. Ma'ṣūmī in his article "Ṣadr al-Dīn al-Shīrāzī" mentions twenty-four commentaries upon it by well-known *ḥakīms* of the subcontinent.
26. Corbin, *Le livre des penetrations métaphysiques*, p. 38; see also Corbin, *Annuaire 1963–64, Ecole Pratique des Hautes Etudes, Section des Sciences Religieuses*, Paris, 1963, pp. 73–7.
27. *Mullā Ṣadrā Commemoration Volume*, p. 33 of the English and p. 26 of the Persian.

28. Mullā Ṣadrā has also commented upon other *ḥadīths* in independent sections of some of his other works. See for example, Ḥā'irī, *Fihrist* . . . vol. IX, part II, p. 950, for the commentary upon the *ḥadīth, kuntu kanzan makhfiyyan* . . . (I was a hidden treasure. . .).
29. Corbin has made a study of these glosses in his "Le thème de la résurrection chez Mollā Ṣadrā Shīrāzī (1050/1640) commentateur de Sohrawardī (587/1191)". *Studies in Mysticism and Religion presented to G. Scholem*, Jerusalem, 1967, pp. 71–115.

Chapter 3

The *Asfār*

The most monumental work of Mullā Ṣadrā, *The Transcendent Theosophy concerning the Four Intellectual Journeys of the Soul*, which we will mention henceforth in the abbreviated and commonly known form of *Asfār*, was completed in its first form in 1037/1628. It stands as the veritable crown of nearly a millennium of Islamic intellectual life, and for Persia and an important section of Muslims of the Indian subcontinent as the fountainhead of their spiritual achievements. A work that has remained virtually unknown to the outside world until modern times, it was mistaken by even such famous students of Persia as Comte de Gobineau and E.G. Browne in the first case for a travelogue and in the second for a collection of "four books"[1] (the term *asfār*, plural of *safar* meaning "journey", having been mistaken for the plural form *asfār* from *sifr*, meaning "book" and derived from the Hebrew *sefer*). It took several more decades and a more intimate acquaintance with the writings of Mullā Ṣadrā to discover even the meaning of the title of this work, not to speak of its content. After years of study of Islamic philosophy and especially of the *ḥakīms* of Persia, H. Corbin could write of the *Asfār* that it is "the great work of Mullā Ṣadrā, the philosophic *summa* of Shī'ite Iran."[2]

The *Asfār* encompasses nearly all the problems discussed by earlier schools of Islamic theology, philosophy and Sufism, and in fact requires a knowledge of all these schools in order to be fully understood. To this day in Persia, it remains the most advanced text of Islamic *ḥikmat*, read only after the student has mastered the well-known texts of *kalām*, Peripatetic philosophy and *ishrāqī* theosophy, not to speak of the all-important tenets of gnosis (*'irfān*). Its treatment of most problems combines a morphological and metaphysical approach with a "historical" one, in the sense that first the views of different schools before Mullā Ṣadrā are discussed and analyzed, and only then does the author turn to his own views, which are all provided with the necessary demonstrations and logical proofs. The *Asfār* is therefore an ocean of Islamic metaphysical doctrines and a treasury of Islamic and, even to a certain extent, of Greek intellectual history, revealing the vast knowledge of its author.[3] It shows also that he must have had access to a very rich library, for many references are made in the *Asfār* to sources which have become scarce since the Safavid period and which have been hardly accessible to even the most learned Muslim scholars of these later centuries.

The method of exposition of the *Asfār* is unique in Mullā Ṣadrā's works and in fact in all Islamic philosophy. Not only are the insights and rigor of a metaphysician combined with the meticulous care and exactness of the historian and scholar, but also the intuitions and illuminations of the seer and mystic are intertwined with the acumen and capability for systematic analysis characteristic of the best of logicians. In each discussion, after giving the views of earlier figures, Muslim as well as Greek, he begins to prove his own doctrine through a careful, logical method. But then there suddenly appears the "research inspired by the Throne" (*taḥqīq 'arshī*), a truth that is derived directly from inspiration in which gnostic verities which have descended from above upon the heart of the sage are laid bare.[4] The fabric of the text of the *Asfār* can be said to be woven of these "vertical" flashes of inspiration and "horizontal" logical explanations and deductions, the whole interspersed with statements of the views of earlier traditional authorities which are thoroughly analyzed and only then either agreed upon or rejected. The work thus remains the supreme testament of Mullā Ṣadrā, begun perhaps during the second period of his life but worked upon continuously until his death. His other writings may be said to be so many children born of this mother, each expounding further one of the *Asfār*'s chapters or discussions.

The title *al-Ḥikmat al-muta'āliyah fi'l-asfār al-'aqliyyat al-arba'ah* was chosen carefully by its author and is laden with the deepest symbolic significance. As far as the term *al-ḥikmat al-muta'āliyah* is concerned, which appears both in the title of the book and as the name of the whole school of Mullā Ṣadrā, this was not coined by him but appears already in Dā'ūd al-

Qayṣarī's commentary upon the *Fuṣūṣ al-ḥikam* of Ibn 'Arabī.[5] Mullā Ṣadrā, however, gives it a new and distinct meaning which has since become identified with his school. What we have translated as the "Transcendent Theosophy" must not in any way be confused with the transcendental categories of Kant or the transcendentalism of an Emerson or Thoreau. The doctrines of Mullā Ṣadrā are theosophy rather than philosophy because they are not derived from discursive thought alone but are ultimately the fruit of a vision of the divine order. And this theosophy is transcendent in the true sense of the word because it derives from the knowledge of a world that transcends the ontological status of man in this terrestial state of existence and stands above his everyday state of consciousness.

The phrase "*al-asfār al-'aqliyyat al-arba'ah*" which comprises the rest of the title of this *magnum opus,* indicates through the symbolism of wayfaring the goal of this work, which is to lead man from the state of ignorance to one of illumination and true awareness. The symbolism of wayfaring is universal and found in nearly all religions[6] and the flight of the soul towards God is often expressed in terms of a journey. The very name of Taoism is derived from the Tao or the "way", while in Islam the names for both the Divine Law or *Sharī'ah* and the esoteric way or *Ṭarīqah* mean literally road or path. The Sufis especially have emphasized in their works the symbolism of travelling. Some Sufi works such as the *Conference of the Birds* (*Manṭiq al-ṭayr*) of 'Aṭṭār are based wholly on this symbolism. Ibn 'Arabī even wrote a treatise whose title includes the name "*al-asfār*" and he discusses the meaning of its singular form, *safar,* in his *al-Iṣṭilāḥāt al-ṣūfiyyah.*

Mullā Ṣadrā was fully conscious of this tradition and in fact in the introduction to the *Asfār* mentions that the gnostics undertake four journeys.[8] He, however, uses the symbolism of journey or *safar* to depict the intellectual process whereby man gains perfect knowledge rather than the "existential" transformation alluded to in classical Sufi works. His "*Asfār*" mean the stages in acquiring complete metaphysical knowledge. The meaning of the four journeys upon whose symbolism the whole of the *Asfār* is based has been explained fully by one of the outstanding Persian gnostics of the past century, Āqā Muḥammad Riḍā Qumsha'ī, as follows:[9]

Know that "journey" (*safar*) means going from a residence or place of stay toward a goal by traversing and crossing different phases and stages. It is either outward, which needs no explanation, or spiritual. The latter according to the people of spiritual vision is of four kinds:

The first journey is from the creature (*khalq*) to the Truth or Creator (*Ḥaqq*) through the tearing of the veils of darkness and light that exist between the initiate (*sālik*) and his spiritual reality, which resides eternally with him. Or one could say that it is an ascent from the station of the carnal soul (*nafs*) to the station of the heart (*qalb*), and from the station of the heart to the station of the spirit (*rūḥ*), and from the station of the spirit to the outermost goal (*al-maqṣad al-aqṣā*) and the supreme splendor (*al-bahjat al-kubrā*). . . . The general stations of man consist of these three. And when it is said that there are a thousand veils between the servant and his Lord, it is in reference to these three general stations. If the initiate reaches the Goal, the veils mentioned are lifted; he contemplates the Divine Beauty and he is annihilated in Him. For this reason it is often called the station of annihilation in the Essence (*al-fanā' fi'l-dhāt*), and therein are contained the secret (*al-sirr*), the hidden (*al-khafiy*) and the most hidden (*al-akhfā'*). . . .

In the station of the spirit or intellect (*al-'aql*), a detailed vision of the intelligibles becomes possible and the stations become seven: the station of *nafs*, of *qalb*, of *'aql*, of *rūḥ*, of *sirr*, of *khafiy* and of *akhfā'*. These stations are given these names because these conditions become permanent for the initiate. If they did not become permanent they would not be called station (*maqām*). And they are the stages of devotion and the city of love to which the "ever-living" gnostic, the Mawlā of Rūm [Jalāl al-Dīn Rūmī] refers [in the poem]:

'Aṭṭār has crossed the seven cities of love;
We are still at the turn of a single street.

هفت شهر عشق را عطار گشت　　ما هنوز اندر خم یک کوچه‌ایم

If the initiate becomes annihilated in the Divine, the first journey comes to an end and his being becomes a true being. . . .

Upon ending the first journey the initiate begins the second journey, which is the journey from the Truth to the Truth by the Truth (*min al-ḥaqq ila'l-ḥaqq bi'l-ḥaqq*). This takes place "by the Truth" because the initiate has become a saint (*walī*) and his being has become real being. He begins this journey from the station of the Essence and goes to the Perfections one after another until he contemplates all the Divine Perfections and knows all the Divine Names except that over which he has no dominance. His sainthood becomes perfect and his essence, actions and qualities become annihilated in the Divine Essence, Actions and Qualities. He hears through His Hearing, sees through His Sight, walks by His Aid and strikes through His Striking. The *sirr* is the annihilation of his essence,the *khafiy* or (the more hidden), the annihilation of his qualities and actions and the *akhfā'* or (the most hidden), the annihilation of these two annihilations. Or one could say that the *sirr* is annihilation in the Essence, which is the end of the first journey and the beginning of the second journey. *Khafiy* is the annihilation in the Divinity (*al-ulūhiyyah*) and the *akhfā'* is the annihilation of these two annihilations, and therein ends the "cycle of initiation" (*dā'irat al-wilāyah*) and the second journey. His annihilation is terminated and the third journey begins.

The third journey is the journey from the Truth to the creature with the Truth (*min al-ḥaqq ila'l-khalq bi'l-ḥaqq*). The initiate journeys at this stage through the states of actions. His annihilation comes to an end and he attains complete sobriety. He subsists through the subsistence (*baqā'*) of God. He journeys through the worlds of *jabarūt*, *malakūt* and *nāsūt* and "sees" all these worlds in their essence and exigencies. He gains a taste of "prophecy" and gains knowledge of the divine sciences from the Divine Essence, Attributes and Actions. But he does *not* possess the prophetic function in the sense of bringing a sacred law. He only brings tidings concerning God, His Attributes and Actions. He is not called a prophet; rather he follows the injunctions and laws of the absolute prophet and is obedient to him. Here ends the third journey and begins the fourth.

The fourth journey is the journey from the creature to the creature with the Truth (*min al-khalq ila'l-khalq bi'l-ḥaqq*). He observes creatures and their effects and exigencies. He knows their benefits and their evils, temporally and spiritually, that is, in this world and the next. He knows of their return to God, the manner of their return. . . . He becomes a prophet in the sense of a law-giving prophet and is called prophet (*nabī*). He brings knowledge of the subsistence of creatures, their harms, their benefits, what causes them to possess felicity and what brings them misery. In all this he is "with the Truth" because his being has become "veridical" and the attention paid by him to the creature does not distract his concentration upon the Divine. . . .

The outstanding philosophers and steadfast sages meditate upon the horizons and their own being and see His portents manifested therein. . . . They prove from the effects of His Power the necessity of His Being and His Essence. . . . They see all existence and all Perfection drowned in His Being and His Perfection. Or rather, they see all existence and perfection as a spark of His Light and a theophany from the theophanies of His Manifestation. This is the first of the four intellectual journeys corresponding to what exists for the initiates among the "people of God" (*ahl Allāh*) and it is from the creature to the Truth.

Then they look at Being and meditate upon Its very reality. It becomes clear to them that It is necessary (*wājib*) in Itself and for Itself and they argue from Its essential necessity to prove that It is without parts, has Unity and possesses Knowledge, Power, Life, Will, Hearing, Sight, Speech and other attributes of Its perfection. . . . This is the second of the four intellectual journeys corresponding to what exists for initiates and it is from the Truth to the Truth by the Truth.

Then they meditate upon His Being, Providence and Unity and the unity of His Act and the process of the effusion of multiplicity from Him – Exalted be He – and its order until the chains of the celestial intellects (*'uqūl*) and the souls (*nufūs*) as ordered become revealed to them. They contemplate the worlds of *jabarūt* and *malakūt* from the highest to the lowest stages until they end with the world of *mulk* and *nāsūt*. . . . And this is the third of the four intellectual journeys corresponding to what exists for those journeying upon the Path. It is from the Truth to the creature with the Truth.

Then they meditate upon the creation of the heavens and the earth. They know of their return to God and possess the science concerning their harms and their benefits, of what is of joy or misery to them in this world and the next. They know of their life and their resurrection. They interdict that which corrupts and order that which is beneficial. They meditate upon the problem of the other world and know what exists therein of heaven and hell, reward and punishment, the path, the account, the balance. . . . This is the fourth of the four intellectual journeys corresponding to what exists for the "people of God" and it is from the creature to the creature with the Truth.

In the book [the *Asfār*] the discussion of general principles and substances and accidents corresponds to the first journey. That dealing with the proof of the Divine Essence through His Essence and the proof of His Attributes corresponds to the second journey. What exists therein concerning the proof of the spiritual substances and the separate souls corresponds to the third journey. And that which concerns the states of the soul and what it undergoes on the Day of Judgment corresponds to the fourth journey.

The *Asfār* then is a complete intellectual journey, which carries the mind through the stages of separation from imperfection, or catharsis (*tajrīd*), to the contemplation of the Divine and from there to the created order seen from a purely metaphysical point of view in the true sense of that word. Hence even natural philosophy and phychology are seen in the mirror of metaphysical truths. Such a vast program naturally requires extensive preparation, hence the years of study of logic, *kalām*, Peripatetic philosophy, *ishrāqī* theosophy and Sufism that are needed before one can embark upon the study of the *Asfār* itself. Moreover, the study of this work itself requires a long period of effort. As taught to the most advanced students in traditional circles, it usually takes six years to teach the work, even though the "journey" or book dealing with natural philosophy (*al-'ilm al-ṭabī'ī*) and usually called the book on substances and accidents (*al-jawāhir wa'l-a'rāḍ*) is not normally taught in regular teaching sessions. There have always been few students who have been capable of grasping all the pearls of this vast ocean of wisdom and few masters who have been competent to unravel all of its mysteries. The title of "teacher of the *Asfār*" (*mudarris-i Asfār*) has been a great honor in Persia not bestowed on everyone. Today in Persia one could not name more than a handful who have real mastery over the whole text and who can explain all of the difficulties which lie hidden behind the façade of a lucid and simple language.[10]

As far as the content of this vast intellectual exposition is concerned, it can best be described by remaining faithful to Mullā Ṣadrā's own treatment of the subject in the *Asfār*, although some problems are treated more than once by him.[11] Hence to understand certain of his arguments and conclusions and to enumerate all of the questions discussed by him it is necessary to connect several sections of the *Asfār* and group under a single heading discussions that belong to one subject but are scattered.

The *Asfār* begins with an introduction of great significance for an understanding of Mullā Ṣadrā himself, for in it he discusses the inner experiences which led him gradually to the discovery of the "Transcendent Theosophy". He also describes in a vivid, literary style the social pressures which he underwent and the difficulties which were placed in his way by some of the jurists and exoteric religious authorities. The introduction of the *Asfār* must be classed with the *Sih aṣl* as being above all a spiritual autobiography.

The first "journey" or *safar*, which is devoted to metaphysics and ontology, consists again of an introduction on the meaning of philosophy, its divisions and purpose, followed by ten parts called *marāḥil* (plural of *marḥalah*), meaning literally stages. The first *marḥalah* is in turn divided into three *manāhij* (plural of *minhaj*) meaning ways or roads, and each *minhaj* in turn into several chapters (*fuṣūl*, plural of *faṣl*). The first *minhaj* deals with being in its essence and prepares the metaphysical and ontological foundation of the whole book. The second and third *manāhij* deal with different qualifications and states of being, including the distinction, going back to Ibn Sīnā, between the necessary (*wājib*), contingent (*mumkin*) and impossible (*mumtani'*) being; and with "mental existence" (*wujūd-i dhihnī*), which is a cornerstone of Mullā Ṣadrā's "Transcendent Theosophy" not found in early Muslim Peripatetic philosophy. The second *marḥalah* continues the discussion of principles pertaining to being and non-being and is in reality an extension of the first.

The third *marḥalah* is concerned with the important problem of *ja'l*, or the effect left by the cause upon that which is caused, which naturally brings with it the question of causality. Also the question of the gradation of being and the stages of "strength" and "weakness" of the light of being are discussed in the last two chapters of this part.

Having discussed being, Mullā Ṣadrā now turns in *marḥalah* four to the question of quiddity (*māhiyyah*) and to the various logical categories that pertain to it. Hence the problem of genus, species and specific difference is discussed and from there the author is led to the question of the relation of form to matter and finally in the last *faṣl* of this part to Platonic ideas. This is a question to which Mullā Ṣadrā returns again and again throughout the *Asfār*.

The fifth *marḥalah* returns once again to questions which concern being and analyzes in detail the connection between unity and multiplicity, the meaning of their opposition and relation. This same concern is reflected in the sixth *marḥalah*, which deals with cause and effect. This is one of the longest sections of the *Asfār* and one of the most gnostic (*'irfānī*) in color. It is more than anything a veiling in a logical thought of a vision of the interrelation of all things with each other and their subordination to and ontological dependence upon the One.

The seventh and eighth *marāḥil* concern motion, the seventh dealing mostly with the Prime-Mover and Its relation to the "moved", and the eighth with motion in general. This in turn leads to the question of the relation between the transient and the permanent and creation in general, which forms the subject of the ninth *marḥalah*.

The first *safar* ends with yet another long section, the tenth *marḥalah*, dealing with the intellect and the intelligible, in which the whole question of knowledge, the relation between the intellect and the intelligible and between the knower and the known, and the stages of knowledge are thoroughly examined.

The second *safar*, dealing with "natural philosophy", makes a study of this subject under the heading of the different traditional categories of Aristotelian logic. Hence the book is divided into an introduction (*muqaddimah*) dealing with the definition of the ten categories and into several chapters called *funūn* (plural of *fann*, meaning "art"), in this case dealing extensively with the separate categories. The first chapter (*fann*) deals with quantity (*kamm*), its different classifications, extension, space, the question of the existence of the vacuum, etc. The second chapter is the most extensive of this *safar*, dealing with quality (*kayf*) and its four-fold division. Under this heading such questions as the different tangible, visible and audible qualities, potentiality, the qualities connected with the soul (*nafs*), qualities connected with quantity such as circularity, geometric form, etc. are considered. Finally the third chapter deals with all the other categories in such a manner that in each case questions dealing with "natural philosophy" are treated. The fourth chapter turns to the question of substance, its classification, bodies, their characteristics, *hylé* and form, etc. In this chapter, more than in any other, is to be found an exposition of Mullā Ṣadrā's physics. The fifth chapter discusses the transient nature of the physical world and its continuous renewal. The problem of creation *ex nihilo* and the eternity of the world is discussed taking into consideration the views of the ancient philosophers, many of whom, like Thales, Anaximenes, Empedocles, Pythagoras, Socrates, Plato and Aristotle, are mentioned by name. Likewise the views of the "people of illumination and gnostic vision" from among the saints and mystics concerning the passing away of material existence are discussed separately. Finally the sixth chapter of this *safar* discusses in a remarkable fashion the relation of nature to its metaphysical principles, its quality of passivity and receptivity before the effusions of the spiritual world, the nexus that connects all natural phenomena to the divine order, and the hierarchy in the natural world, which is directly related to the degree of receptivity of things to Divine grace.

Having dealt with "natural philosophy", Mullā Ṣadrā now turns in the third *safar* to the science dealing with the Divine Essence, Names and Qualities, the science which in traditional Islamic parlance is called "metaphysics in its particular sense" (*al-ilāhiyyāt bi'l-ma'na'l-akhaṣṣ)* and which may be translated as theodicy. This book consists of ten *mawāqif* (plural of *mawqif* meaning literally "stopping place"), which cover all the aspects of theodicy considered in different traditional sources. The first *mawqif* deals with God as the Necessary Being (*wājib al-wujūd*), the different proofs given for His Existence, His Unity and the "Simplicity" of His Essence. In this section special attention is paid to the views of the *ḥakīms* immediately preceding Mullā Ṣadrā, especially Jalāl al-Dīn Dawānī and Sayyid Ṣadr al-Dīn Shīrāzī, the latter of whom many have mistaken for Mullā Ṣadrā himself. The second *mawqif* concerns the Divine Qualities, both the affirmative (*thubūtiyyah*) and the negative (*salbiyyah*), and the relation of the Qualities to the Divine Essence. In the long and very important third *mawqif*, Mullā Ṣadrā turns to the difficult question of God's knowledge of the world. The views of nearly all the earlier schools of philosophy, *kalām* and Sufism are outlined and discussed and Mullā Ṣadrā finally offers his own well-known theory, which represents one of the outstanding features of the "Transcendent Theosophy" and which is based on the idea that God's knowledge of things is their very reality or being.

Having discussed the Quality of knowledge (*'ilm*), Mullā Ṣadrā turns in the fourth *mawqif* to the other primary Divine Quality of power (*qudrah*), or to the question of how the Divine Will acts in creation. The long dispute between the philosophers and Ash'arite theologians on the question of Divine Will and its relation to knowledge is also fully discussed. Two short *mawqifs*, the fifth and sixth, deal with two other basic Divine Qualities, Living (*ḥayāt*) and Hearing (*sam'*), while a longer *mawqif*, the seventh, deals with the Divine Quality of Speech (*takallum*), and here the question of revealed books, particularly the Quran and certain of its esoteric aspects, is also discussed. The long eighth *mawqif* deals with providence and how Divine Will and destiny act in this world. In addition to many other basic religious questions, that of good and evil and how there can be evil in the world despite the reign of the Divine Will over all things are analyzed. The signs of Divine Wisdom in creatures, in both the macrocosm and the microcosm, and the love (*'ishq*) which prevades all things are also discussed. The ninth *mawqif* turns to Divine Acts (*af'āl*), hence to creation, the grades of manifestation beginning with the Logos and the intelligible world. The tenth and final *mawqif* concerns the problem of the continuity of Divine Manifestation and the finite, temporal existence of creation, and thus turns again of necessity to the difficult dichotomy between the religious belief in the creation of the world *ex nihilo* and the philosophical view of its "eternity", which is related to the eternal quality of the Divine as source of manifestation and creation. On this question of the relation between the temporal and the eternal or the world and God (*ḥudūth wa qidam*) Mullā Ṣadrā offers once again a profound insight based upon the doctrine of transsubstantial motion which is yet another distinguishing feature of his "Transcendent Theosophy". Throughout this *safar*, intellectual (*'aqlī*) problems are intertwined with those drawn from transmitted (*naqlī*) sources and many of the delicate problems connected with the Quran and *Ḥadīth* are elucidated.

The final book or *safar* of the *Asfār* is devoted to traditional psychology (*'ilm al-nafs*) and eschatology, inasmuch as Mullā Ṣadrā, in eleven chapters, this time entitled *abwāb* (plural of *bāb* meaning "gate"), deals with all the stages of the growth of the soul from the moment the foetus is formed to its ultimate resurrection and encounter with God. It would not be an exaggeration to say that in no other work in Islamic annals has this question been treated so extensively and so profoundly. It combines the systematic treatment of Ibn Sīnā in the sixth book of the *Ṭabī'iyyāt* of the *Shifā'* with the illuminative insights of Ibn 'Arabī in his *al-Futūḥāt al-makkiyyah*, and is connected in substance more to the second than to the first.

The first chapter (*bāb*) of the fourth *safar* begins with the definition of the soul and proofs for its existence. Having proved the existence of the soul, Mullā Ṣadrā then turns in the second *bāb* to the animal soul, for whose independence from matter or "immortality" he argues. The different powers of the animal soul which are connected to the body are also discussed. In a long third chapter an extensive treatment is given of the vegetative soul, all of whose faculties are likewise enumerated and described. In the fourth *bāb* Mullā Ṣadrā turns back to the animal soul and discusses the faculties which belong distinctively to it. The outer senses are described and special attention is paid to the question of vision. Having made clear the function of the outer senses, he then turns in the fifth *bāb* to the inner senses, beginning with the *sensus communis* and proceeding to the other inner faculties of traditional psychology. Mullā Ṣadrā emphasizes especially the unity of the soul and the fact that it possesses all the faculties within itself. He also criticizes certain of the views of Ibn Sīnā on the soul.

In the sixth chapter proof is given of the state of catharsis (*tajarrud*) and complete independence of the soul from matter, while in the seventh chapter Mullā Ṣadrā discusses the relation of the soul to the corporeal world and the difficult problem of the genesis of the soul. In the eighth chapter the views of those who believe in transmigration and similar ideas are discussed and rejected.

The last three chapters of this journey turn to the most sublime questions of the higher states of perfection possible for the human soul, and of spiritual and corporeal resurrection. In the last *bāb*, on bodily resurrection, Mullā Ṣadrā turns to Quranic teachings concerning the afterlife and explains the meaning of the pains or joys of the grave, the resurrection of all things, the Hour, the Trumpet and the minor and major "judgements". The paradisial and infernal states, their meaning, and the stages of perfection leading to the different levels of paradise are also explained. The work ends with a section on the condition of those who dwell in heaven and hell and a quotation drawn from the *al-Futūḥāt al-makkiyyah* of Ibn 'Arabī.

* * *

It is quite natural that this monumental exposition of traditional doctrines should have become the subject of many commentaries. Many of the outstanding *ḥakīms* of the past three centuries have written glosses or commentaries upon parts or in some cases all of the *Asfār*. Some are well-known; others remain hidden, like so many other works of the past few centuries, in corners of libraries in Persia, Pakistan and India, waiting to be studied. Most of the manuscripts of the *Asfār* contain handwritten notes on the margin which reflect the meditations of the teacher or student who has used the manuscript in question. Sometimes the glosses of several generations of *ḥakīms* are recorded in a single manuscript, attesting to the continuous role played by the *Asfār* in the intellectual life of Persia during the past three centuries. Of the better known glosses and commentaries upon the *Asfār*, the following may be singled out: those of Āqā Muḥammad Bīdābādī, Mullā 'Alī Nūrī Iṣfahānī, Mullā Ismā'īl Iṣfahānī, Ḥājjī Mullā Hādī Sabziwārī, Mullā 'Alī Mudarris Zunūzī, Āqā Muḥammad Riḍā Qumsha'ī, Mīrzā Hāshim Gīlānī Rashtī Ashkiwarī, Mullā Āqā Qazwīnī, Mīrzā Muḥammad Hāshim Mūsawī Khwānsārī, Muḥammad ibn Ma'ṣūm Zanjānī and Sayyid Muḥammad Ḥusayn Ṭabāṭabā'ī.[12]

The most extensive glosses upon the *Asfār* are those of Sabziwārī, which embrace the first, third and fourth journeys and were printed in the margin of the lithographed edition of the *Asfār*. After the glosses of Sabziwārī, the most copious are those of Mullā 'Alī Mudarris Zunūzī, which many of the traditional authorities consider the most profound and penetrating commentary yet written upon this work. The glosses of the contemporary *ḥakīm*, Sayyid Muḥammad Ḥusayn Ṭabāṭabā'ī, which appear in the footnotes of the recently printed edition of the *Asfār*, have been written after consultation with most of these older glosses and comprise an important addition to the already imposing list of commentaries upon this remarkable *summa*.

Notes

1. The passages in question are as follows: "Il a écrit de plus quatre livres de voyages." Comte de Gobineau, *Les religions et les philosophies dans l'Asie centrale*, Paris, 1866, p. 81. "The two most celebrated of Mullā Ṣadrā's works . . . are the *Asfār-i Arba'a* or 'Four Books' and the *Shawāhidu'r-Rubūbiyya*. . . ." E.G. Browne, *A Literary History of Persia*, Vol. 4, p. 430.
2. See his introduction to the *Livre des pénétrations métaphysiques*, p. 30.
3. See S.H. Nasr, "Mullā Ṣadrā as a Source for the History of Muslim Philosophy", in *Islamic Studies*, chapter eleven.
4. Concerning the meaning of *'arshī* see the prolegomena of H. Corbin to Suhrawardī, *Opera Metaphysica et Mystica*, vol. I, Tehran, 1976, pp. LIII–LIV.
5. While discussing God's knowledge of things, Qayṣarī refers to

   هـذا و ان كان له وجـه عنده من تعـلم الحكمة الالهيـة المتـعالية مـن المـوحـدين

   Kitāb sharḥ fuṣūṣ al-ḥikam of Qayṣarī, Tehran, 1299 (A.H. lunar), p. 15.
6. See M. Pallis, *The Way and the Mountain*, London, 1960.
7. The work of Ibn 'Arabī in question is *Kitāb al-isfār 'an natā'ij al-asfār*, printed in Hyderabad in 1948. See also pp. 318–19 of vol. I of O. Yahya, *Histoire et classification de l'oeuvre d'Ibn 'Arabī*, Damas, 1963. As for the meaning of *safar*, see *al-Iṣṭilāḥāt al-ṣūfiyyah*, *risālah* no. 29 in *Rasā'il Ibn 'Arabī*, Hyderabad, 1948, p. 2.
8. See *Asfār*, vol. I, p. 13.

   «و اعلم أنّ للسلاک من العرفاء الأولياء أسفاراً أربعة»
9. *Asfār*, vol. I, pp. 13–16.
10. Of the contemporary masters who are outstanding authorities on Mullā Ṣadrā and teachers of the *Asfār*, we must mention especially Ḥaḍrat-i Āyatallāh Sayyid Abu'l-Ḥasan Rafī'ī Qazwīnī and 'Allāmah Sayyid Muḥammad Ḥusayn Ṭabāṭabā'ī, both of whom have trained a whole generation of younger *ḥakīms* in Persia. We have had the rare privilege of studying the *Asfār* and other traditional texts for years with both masters and can attest to their remarkable mastery of the doctrines of Mullā Ṣadrā.
11. The headings of the chapters of the *Asfār* and their pagination according to the lithographed edition have been given by M.I. Āyatī, "*Fihrist-i abwāb wa fuṣūl-i kitāb-i asfār*", *Mullā Ṣadrā Commemoration Volume*, pp. 63–106.
12. The *Asfār* has always been studied in its Arabic version and all of the glosses mentioned here are in Arabic. During this century, however, attempts have been made to make the contents of the *Asfār* available in Persian and Urdu. A summary of the first and third journeys of the *Asfār* with explanations and a translation of the fourth *safar* has been given by J. Muṣliḥ in his *Falsafa-yi 'ālī yā ḥikmat-i Ṣadr al-muta'allihīn* (see Chapter 2, page 39). An Urdu translation of the first *safar* was made by Sayyid Manāẓir Aḥsan Gīlānī in two volumes, Hyderabad, 1941–42.

Chapter 4

The Sources of Mullā Sadrā's Doctrines and Ideas

In discussing the "sources" of the doctrines and ideas of Mullā Ṣadrā, it is essential to inquire first of all into the meaning of the word "source", for we are not dealing here with just historical causes and influences and cannot reduce Mullā Ṣadrā's intellectual vision to the simple amalgamation of a certain number of previously existing ideas. No amount of historical research will enable us to discover all of his "sources" in writings belonging to periods before him, for such a figure cannot be reduced to the "effect" of a number of historical causes. To be sure, Mullā Ṣadrā drank deeply from the fountainhead of Islamic wisdom and drew on the writings of numerous sages and philosophers before him, both Islamic and pre-Islamic. But one can always observe in his doctrines the presence of the element of inspiration (*ilhām*) and intuition (*dhawq*), or a "vertical cause" which transforms constantly the very substance of the ideas received from earlier sages and philosophers into the elements of a new metaphysical vision of things.

Mullā Ṣadrā founded a new intellectual school in Islam, which means that he was able to open up a new perspective. But because his was a *traditional* theosophy, and not an individualistic creation, it can also be said that, essentially, he reiterated the same eternal truth which other sages had formulated in other ways before him. His "Transcendent Theosophy" is yet another version of the *philosophia perennis,* but one which is particularly rich in that it encompasses nearly all the traditional sciences of Islam. There was, to be sure, adaptation and borrowing from earlier sources, as the very notion of "tradition" itself implies and necessitates, but there is always a "re-creation" and transmutation which makes earlier material appear in a new light. This light did not come simply from borrowing from earlier works but resulted from the illumination of Mullā Ṣadrā's being and intellect and from inspiration received from on high, an inspiration which he usually refers to as coming from the Divine Throne (*al-'arsh*).

There have been a few scholars who, influenced by the crass historicism of so much modern Western, and now sometimes Eastern scholarship, have attempted to "trace back" Mullā Ṣadrā's writings to their original sources with the insinuation that he simply borrowed from these sources without acknowledging his debt.[1] These authors forget first of all that in traditional sciences it is customary to cite earlier works, which are usually known to scholars, without mentioning the name of the author; secondly that the mere fact that the traces of an idea, such as for example the unity of the instrument of intellection and the intelligible (*ittiḥād al-'āqil wa'l-ma'qūl*), are found in some previous writing does not diminish the significance of the vast development that that idea has undergone in the writings of Ṣadr al-Dīn and the significance such an idea has gained in the total scheme of things as conceived by him; and thirdly that Ṣadr al-Dīn, like so many other traditional Muslim scholars, was deeply impregnated with the teaching contained in the famous saying of 'Alī, "Pay attention to what is said, not to who has said it".[2]

If one is to discuss the "sources" of Mullā Ṣadrā, at least in their historical aspect, it is essential to keep in mind the traditional character of the teachings in question, therefore the importance of truth over originality, the sense of belonging to a spiritual universe which embraces other sages who come before Mullā Ṣadrā and finally the synthesizing power of Ṣadr al-Dīn, who sought consciously to unite together the different Islamic intellectual schools that preceded him. It is also important to distinguish between those writings of Ṣadr al-Dīn, especially the *Asfār,* in which on purpose many different Muslim sources are deliberately cited in order to be discussed or refuted and works in which only his own ideas are expounded.

When in full consideration of all of these factors a study is made of the writings of Mullā Ṣadrā with an awareness of his genius as well as of his intellectual tradition, it becomes immediately clear that besides being an outstanding metaphysician, he was a remarkable scholar who had read widely as far as various fields of Islamic learning are concerned.[3] This fact was recognized even before modern times by many of the traditional *ḥakīms* of Persia, some of whom in fact sought to trace back the sources of some of the sections of the *Asfār* to earlier Islamic works and to show Mullā Ṣadrā's relation to the important intellectual figures before him.[4] Mullā Ṣadrā's remarkable breadth as well as depth of knowledge of earlier sources and the phenomenal memory which he must have had have been a source of wonder to all generations of later *ḥakīms,* not to speak of contemporary scholars. All who know his works acknowledge the fact that no Muslim *ḥakīm* was ever as widely read as he and no work on *ḥikmat* is as rich a source of Islamic philosophy, theology and gnosis as the *Asfār.*

In turning to the main sources of a traditional and at the same time "historical" order which provided the elements for Mullā Ṣadrā's "Transcendent Theosophy", we must begin with the sources of the Islamic tradition itself, namely the Quran and *Ḥadīth.* There is perhaps no other Muslim philosopher and *ḥakīm* who knew the Quran as well as Mullā Ṣadrā. It is true that Ibn Sīnā wrote some commentaries upon various Quranic verses,[5] and that Suhrawardī was the first Muslim theosopher to bring Quranic verses as evidence for his philosophical and theosophical expositions. But none of the earlier *ḥakīms* were as well acquainted with the intricacies of the text of the Holy Quran and the whole tradition of later commentaries written upon it as Ṣadr al-Dīn. In unveiling the inner meaning of the Holy Quran, Ṣadr al-Dīn belongs more to the line of Ibn 'Arabī, 'Abd al-Razzāq Kāshānī and other outstanding gnostic commentators and masters of spiritual hermeneutics (*ta'wīl*) than to the school of philosophers. His studies of the inner meaning of the Quran are so vast as to merit a separate study. But the influence of the Quran upon him is not limited to his formal commentaries. Quranic verses abound in all of his writings and the spirit and light of the Quran shine through practically every page of his works. Without the direct influence of the Quran his writings would not be conceivable.[6]

Ṣadr al-Dīn was also well versed in the literature of *Ḥadīth,* Sunni and Shi'ite alike, and quoted not only Shi'ite authorities but occasionally Sunni transmitters such as Ibn 'Abbās as well. As far as the Shi'ite corpus of *Ḥadīth* is concerned, the intimate relation between his doctrines and this corpus is best revealed in his uncompleted commentary upon the *Uṣūl al-kāfī* of Kulaynī, which is one of his masterpieces. But in his other writings as well there are often references to the more sapiential and esoteric *ḥadīths* drawn not only from Kulaynī but also from such sources as the *Kitāb al-tawḥīd, Kitāb al-i'tiqādāt* and *Ma'ānī al-akhbār* of Ibn Bābūyah, known also as Shaykh-i Ṣadūq. Like all things Islamic, the "Transcendent Theosophy" of Mullā Ṣadrā draws upon the *Ḥadīth* as a second source which complements the message of the Quran. For Ṣadr al-Dīn the *Ḥadīth,* like the Quran, possesses several levels of esoteric meaning which can be reached only with the aid of that inner illumination that first reveals to the seeker the inner layers of his own being before unveiling before him the inner sense of the sacred text.

Mullā Ṣadrā was likewise well acquainted with other types of strictly religious writings, especially theology (*Kalām*), whose arguments he knew thoroughly. He studied this science with an open eye, and without the violent opposition seen among so many of the other *falāsifah.* He sometimes rejected its teachings and at other times integrated its doctrines into his own world view.[7] It is of special interest to note that although thoroughly impregnated with Shi'ite thought, Mullā Ṣadrā knew Sunni *kalām* as intimately as the Shi'ite. Such classical Ash'arite authors as Ash'arī himself, Ghazzālī, Fakhr al-Dīn Rāzī and 'Aḍud al-Dīn Ījī are cited often by Mulla Ṣadrā who was also aware of differences of opinion between the theologians, especially between the views of Ghazzālī and Fakhr al-Dīn Rāzī and their respective roles in the history of Islamic philosophy. In this category, he made extensive use especially of the writings of Fakhr al-Dīn whose *al-Mabāḥith al-mashriqiyyah,* itself a compendium of early Islamic thought, is a major source of Mullā Ṣadrā's knowledge of early schools of *kalām* and philosophy. The *Sharḥ al-mawāqif* of Jurjānī must also be singled out as a theological work whose influence in Ṣadr al-Dīn's writings is quite discernible.

Mullā Ṣadrā was also familiar with the Mu'tazilite school, many of whose early masters he quotes in the *Asfār.* The presence of certain Mu'tazilite theses can be seen in Ṣadr al-Dīn's writings both directly through Mu'tazilite texts and indirectly through Shi'ite sources. But altogether Ash'arite theology seems to play a more dominant role in the intellectual discussions of the *Asfār* and the other works of Mullā Ṣadrā than Mu'tazilite thought.

As for Shi'ite theology, it was naturally the *Tajrīd* of Naṣīr al-Dīn Ṭūsī, with all of its famous commentaries and glosses by such men as 'Allāmah Ḥillī, Shams al-Dīn Khafrī, Fakhr al-Dīn

Sammâkī, Ṣadr al-Dīn Dashtakī and Ghiyāth al-Dīn Manṣūr Dashtakī, which served as the main source for Mullā Ṣadrā's knowledge in this field. He was thoroughly acquainted with the vast literature that had come into being around this basic text from the time of Ṭūsī until his own day, a corpus which belongs in a sense as much to the domain of philosophy as to *kalām*. Moreover, Mullā Ṣadrā shows familiarity with other Shi'ite theological works of a philosophical and mystical nature of the ninth/fifteenth and tenth/sixteenth century, works of such men as Jalāl al-Dīn Dawānī, the Dashtakī family and Sayyid Ḥaydar Āmulī. That type of Shi'ite theological writing which began to employ the methods of philosophical demonstration and to concern itself with the different themes of traditional philosophy, or which sought to combine gnosis and Sufism with *kalām*, is one of the pillars upon which Mullā Ṣadrā built his vast intellectual edifice.

Mullā Ṣadrā's knowledge of Shi'ite *kalām* extended also to the Ismā'īlī branch of Shi'ism, where *kalām* and a particular form of philosophy had developed from an early period of Islamic history.[8] Among the Ismā'īlī authors, Mullā Ṣadrā was influenced particularly by Ḥamīd al-Dīn Kirmānī and his *Rāḥat al-'aql* and also by the *Rasā'il* of the Ikhwān al-Ṣafā', which, although perhaps not written definitely by Ismā'īlī authors, became integrated later into Ismā'īlī religious literature.[9] In such questions as the "flow of existence" (*sarayān al-wujūd*) within all things, the infusion of the power of nature within the corporeal world and the creation of the soul with the body, Ḥamīd al-Dīn's influence on Mullā Ṣadrā is quite discernible. As for the *Rasā'il,* it is in the combining of Quranic verses with philosophical questions, the discussion of the universal power of love, certain eschatological problems and the comparison between the microcosm and macrocosm that striking parallels are to be found with the works of Ṣadr al-Dīn.

Turning to the esoteric teachings of Islam contained in Sufism, one is startled to discover Mullā Ṣadrā's acquaintance with the whole mainstream of Sufism. The writings of Mullā Ṣadrā are as deeply influenced by the Sufi tradition as can be imagined, both "horizontally" and historically, through his acquaintance with earlier Sufi writings, and "vertically", through contact with the Truth (*al-ḥaqīqah*), which is itself the eternal source of all Sufism. Ṣadr al-Dīn knew nearly all types of Sufi literature. He often quotes the early Sufi texts of an ethical and operative nature such as the *Qūt al-qulūb, Manāzil al-sā'irīn, 'Awārif al-ma'ārif* and *Iḥyā' 'ulūm al-dīn,* whose effect upon Mullā Ṣadrā is particularly notable.[10] He also shows knowledge of the more theoretical Sufi works such as the *Zubdah* of 'Ayn al-Quḍāt Hamadānī and the writings of 'Alā' al-Dawlah Simnānī.

Mullā Ṣadrā also knew intimately the tradition of Persian Sufi poetry in one of whose centers, Shiraz, he had in fact been raised. But within the Persian cultural world it is the *Mathnawī* of Mawlānā Jalāl al-Dīn Rūmī that is quoted most often by him. Many of its verses adorn his writings and he often turns to this inexhaustible treasury of wisdom to demonstrate through a beautiful verse some particular intellectual argument he has tried to prove through logical demonstration. In the spirituality characteristic of Ṣadr al-Dīn, both the Sufism of the type of Rūmī and that of Ibn 'Arabī and his followers meet. It is no wonder that Ṣadr al-Dīn's most famous follower during the succeeding centuries, namely Ḥājjī Mullā Hādī Sabziwārī, while being deeply influenced, like his master, by Muḥyī al-Dīn, also wrote a commentary upon the *Mathnawī*.

Despite the significance of Rūmī and other masters, however, it is the Sufism of the school of Ibn 'Arabī that has left the most profound mark upon Ṣadr al-Dīn, whose works contain literally hundreds of references to this Andalusian master of Islamic gnosis. Mullā Ṣadrā quotes most often from the *Fuṣūṣ al-ḥikam* and the *al-Futūḥāt al-makkiyyah,* especially in questions of eschatology. In fact, as already mentioned (see p. 64), the last part of the *Asfār* dealing with the soul and its becoming terminates with a long passage from the *Futūḥāt.* Mullā Ṣadrā would be inconceivable without Ibn 'Arabī, and one of the most important radii of influence of the teachings of Shaykh al-Akbar must be sought in Mullā Ṣadrā and his school.[11]

Besides Ibn 'Arabī, his disciples and the major commentators were also well known to Mullā Ṣadrā. In the *Asfār* there are references to Dā'ūd al-Qayṣarī, one of the principal commentators of the *Fuṣūṣ,* as well as to Ḥamzah Fanārī and his *Nafaḥāt* and Ṣadr al-Dīn al-Qunyawī and his *Mafātīḥ al-ghayb,* both of which belong integrally to the school of Ibn 'Arabī. Few intellectual masters of Islam knew Ibn 'Arabī as well as Mullā Ṣadrā and it is mostly through his writings that the influence of Ibn 'Arabī reached later generations of Persian *ḥakīms* and gnostics (*'ārifs*).

In the domain of philosophy itself, the acquaintance of Mullā Ṣadrā with the different schools, both Islamic and pre-Islamic, is also truly astonishing. Among the Greek and Alexandrian schools, he cites sources ranging from the Pre-Socratics, through Plato and Aristotle to the Neoplatonists and even Stoics. Of special interest, however, is Mullā Ṣadrā's respect for the Pre-Socratics, which results from his intimate knowledge of the *ishrāqī* tradition and thought. He must have known the wealth of material relating to the Pre-Socratics in Arabic anthologies such as those of Ibn Hindū and Ibn al-Fātik. At times also he gives the profoundest interpretation of the teachings of these Greek sages; for instance, when he interprets the water of Thales as the prime psycho-spiritual substance of the cosmos and not just as a physical element, and identifies this water with the "Breath of the Compassionate" (*nafas al-raḥmān*) of the Sufis.[12]

Among the Pre-Socratics he reserves a special place for Pythagoras, whom he upholds as a model of a sage and theosopher, again following the example of Suhrawardī and the *ishrāqīs*. One can find references to the *Golden Verses* (which he calls *al-Risālat al-dhahabiyyah*) in Mullā Ṣadrā's writings. The Pythagorean vein in his teachings can be traced in fact not only to *ishrāqī* elements but also to such works as the *Rasā'il* of the Ikhwān al-Ṣafā'. On the purely metaphysical plane, this Pythagorean color is due to an inner sympathy and attraction in Islam for Pythagorean doctrines, which early in the life of Islamic civilization became integrated into certain dimensions of Islamic esotericism. The mathematical symbolism, harmony and unity of Pythagorean wisdom resembled morphologically the metaphysical structure of Islam in which harmony and unity as well as mathematical symbolism play such an important role.[13]

As for Plato, Mullā Ṣadrā again displays a remarkable understanding of many of his ideas and discusses extensively in the *Asfār* and elsewhere some of his basic theses, such as the "Platonic ideas" and the concept of space. As with other Muslim philosophers, it was mainly from the *Timaeus* that Mullā Ṣadrā drew his knowledge of Platonic philosophy. But without doubt he also knew some of the other Platonic *Dialogues* and in fact refers directly to the *Phaedo* in the *Asfār*.

Like his Muslim predecessors, Mullā Ṣadrā was more acquainted with Aristotle than with other Greek philosophers, but with an Aristotle who was really more Plotinus and Proclus than the Stagirite. Doubtless Mullā Ṣadrā knew as much of Aristotle as the early Muslim Peripatetics and therefore had studied in detail the *Metaphysics, Physics, On the Soul,* etc. But the "Aristotle" quoted most often by Mullā Ṣadrā is the author of *al-Ma'rifat al-rubūbiyyah* (*On Divine Knowledge*), the *Uthūlūjiyā* (*Theology*) and *Kitāb al-tafāḥah* (*Liber de Pomo*), all of which are connected with Neoplatonism. As in the case of most early Muslim philosophers, the acquaintance of Mullā Ṣadrā with "Aristotelian" sources embraces Neoplatonism as well.

Mullā Ṣadrā was also influenced to a certain extent by some of the motifs of Stoic logic and natural philosophy, probably through such indirect sources as the writings of Galen. But what is most curious is his use of the word Stoic (*riwāqī*) in a manner which is the culmination of a tradition that antedates him by some centuries. Despite several recent studies on Stoicism in Islam,[14] it is not as yet known how the term *riwāqī* gradually came to mean in the later schools of Islamic philosophy the most exalted and sublime theosophy standing above not only the Peripatetic but occasionally also the Illuminationist school. This is all the more strange in that Stoicism, at least of the type found in the ancient world, was especially known for its lack of interest in metaphysics and gnosis. But Mullā Ṣadrā refers often in his *Asfār* and elsewhere to three orders of *ḥakīms*: the Peripatetics (*mashshā'ī*), the Illuminationists (*ishrāqī*) and the Stoics (*riwāqī*). At other times he uses *riwāqī* as if it were synonymous with *ishrāqī*.[15] However, until extensive research clarifies the way in which *riwāqī* came to acquire such a meaning for Mullā Ṣadrā and other theosophers of his school, the mere use of the word *riwāqī* in his writings should not be seen as indicating a connection with Stoicism. The connection of Mullā Ṣadrā's ideas to Stoic sources must be gauged from the substance of the ideas under discussion rather than from the use of the term *riwāqī* with all the meaning that it acquired during the later history of Islamic philosophy.[16]

Mullā Ṣadrā's knowledge of earlier Islamic philosophy was of course much more thorough and complete than his acquaintance with Greek sources.[17] In the history of the Peripatetic school, Mullā Ṣadra knew al-Kindī and was aware of his solution to the problem of the relation between religion and philosophy, or revelation and reason, but rarely did he refer to his works. Al-Fārābī, however, was more familiar to him and he quotes him often, especially the *Fuṣūl* and the *Fuṣūṣ al-ḥikam*. Mullā Ṣadrā also knew well Abu'l-Ḥasan al-'Āmirī, whose writings gradually receded from the mainstream of Islamic intellectual life and are only now being brought once again into light. Mullā Ṣadrā, however, recognized 'Āmirī as a major intellectual figure and quotes from time to time from such works of 'Āmirī as *al-Amad 'ala'l-abad,* a history of philosophy that has not as yet even been edited and printed in modern times.

Naturally Mullā Ṣadrā's knowledge of Peripatetic philosophy is most extensive and detailed when we come to the writings of Ibn Sīnā. Besides the purely religious sources, namely the Quran and *Ḥadīth,* Ibn Sīnā must be considered, along with Suhrawardī and Ibn 'Arabī, as Mullā Ṣadrā's most important source. Not only did Ṣadr al-Dīn know intimately practically every line and word of Ibn Sīnā's well-known philosophical works, such as the *Shifā',*[18] the *Najāt, al-Mabda' wa'l-ma'ād, Risālah fi'l-'ishq* and *'Uyūn al-ḥikmah,*[19] but he also quoted often from some of Ibn Sīnā's important but recently neglected works such as the *Ta'līqāt*[20] and the *Mubāḥathāt.* Mullā Ṣadrā also knew the writings of Ibn Sīnā's students, such as Bahmanyār, whose *Taḥṣīl* and *al-Bahjah wa'l-sa'ādah* he quoted. He also knew Bahmanyār's student, Abu'l-'Abbās Lūkarī. As for the later Peripatetics, Mullā Ṣadrā shows familiarity with *Kitāb al-mu'tabar* of Abu'l-Barakāt al-Baghdādī. But his special attention is devoted to Naṣir al-Din Ṭūsī, who revived Ibn Sīnā's philosophy. Mullā Ṣadrā called Ṭūsī the person upon whose shoulders the "Throne of Philosophy" stands and always showed the greatest reverence for him. The important philosophical works of Ṭūsī such as the *Sharḥ al-ishārāt wa'l-tanbīhāt, Risālat al-'ilm* and *Mulakhkhaṣ,* also known as *Naqd al-muḥaṣṣal,* were well known to Mullā Ṣadrā. Likewise he knew the Peripatetic works of Naṣīr al-Dīn's students and of those around him, such as the *Durrat al-tāj* of Quṭb al-Dīn Shīrāzī, the *Ḥikmat al-'ayn* of Dabīrān Kātibī Qazwīnī and the *Hidāyah* of Athīr al-Dīn Abharī, upon which in fact Mullā Ṣadrā wrote one of his best known works, the *Sharḥ al-hidāyah.* This work became so famous in the Indo-Pakistani subcontinent that it is referred to there as *Ṣadrā.*

The later phase of Peripatetic philosophy, which was closely connected with Shiraz and the Dashtakī family, was also well-known to Mullā Ṣadrā, who refers very often to both Ṣadr al-Dīn and Ghiyāth al-Dīn Manṣūr Dashtakī. Unfortunately until now none of the works of Ghiyāth al-Dīn Manṣūr has been properly edited and printed, so that even in Persia his thought remains nearly unknown. But he is without doubt one of Mullā Ṣadrā's most important immediate predecessors and probably the most notable Peripatetic philosopher after Naṣīr al-Dīn, a remarkable figure who like Naṣīr al-Dīn exercised a profound influence upon Mullā Ṣadrā.[21]

When we come to the writings of the *ishrāqī* school, we find again a profound knowledge of the sources. It was of course Suhrawardī himself from whom Mullā Ṣadrā mostly drew for his knowledge of the *ishrāqī* school. His penetration into the writings and teachings of Suhrawardī can best be seen in his glosses upon the *Ḥikmat al-ishrāq*. In fact Mullā Ṣadrā saw himself as the person who brought to full perfection the theosophical doctrines first expounded by Suhrawardī. His metaphysical exposition can be seen as another version of the world view of Suhrawardī, but interpreted in the light of the doctrine of the principiality of existence (*aṣālat al-wujūd*) rather than the principiality of quiddity (*aṣālat al-māhiyyah*) which was accepted by Suhrawardī. In many ways, however, these two giants of later Islamic intellectual history complement each other; they certainly belong to the same spiritual universe. It is no accident that the highest station of those who seek after knowledge is referred to by Suhrawardī as the station of the *ḥakīm muta'allih* or theosopher,[22] and that Mullā Ṣadrā was given the honorific title *Ṣadr al-muta'allihīn* (foremost among the theosophers), a title which can be understood only in the context of the meaning of *muta'allih* in the school of *ishrāqī* wisdom.

Among the writings of Suhrawardī, Mullā Ṣadrā drew most of all from the *Ḥikmat al-ishrāq* with its commentary by Quṭb al-Dīn Shīrāzī.[23] But he also used other works of Suhrawardī especially the *Talwīḥāt*, the *Muṭāraḥāt* and *Hayākil al-nūr*, to all of which he refers in the *Asfār* and elsewhere. He was acquainted with the works of Suhrawardī's successors, not only Quṭb al-Dīn, but also the much less studied Shams al-Dīn Shahrazūrī, whose important *al-Sharjarat al-ilāhiyyah* and most likely his commentary upon the *Ḥikmat al-ishrāq* were known to Mullā Ṣadrā.

Of the later *ishrāqīs*, Mullā Ṣadrā of course knew well the writings of Jalāl al-Dīn Dawānī and those of Ibn Turkah. Unfortunately as yet no serious study has been made of Ibn Turkah's writings,[24] but any cursory analysis of them will reveal the role played by Ibn Turkah as a major link between Suhrawardī and Mullā Ṣadrā, especially in his attempt to harmonize Peripatetic and *ishrāqī* doctrines with gnosis, thus anticipating the synthesis achieved by Ṣadr al-Dīn.

By far the most influential of the Safavid predecessors of Ṣadr al-Dīn is Mīr Dāmād, the founder of the "School of Isfahan", and Mullā Ṣadrā's teacher. Mīr Dāmād was essentially Avicennian with an *ishrāqī* color and differed in many ways from Mullā Ṣadrā; he nevertheless prepared the way for the appearance of Mullā Ṣadrā, who really represents the crowning achievement of the "School of Isfahan". Mullā Ṣadrā fully understood his master's views and alluded to them throughout his works, especially in the *Asfār.* The work of Mīr Dāmād most often cited is his masterpiece, the *Qabasāt,* where the question of time as well as creation in its relation to time, so central to Mīr Dāmād's whole thought, is thoroughly discussed. Mullā Ṣadrā was also aware of other intellectual figures of the Safavid period, but they were all subordinated to the towering figure of Mīr Dāmād, who was not only his teacher, but also more universally the "Third Teacher" (*al-mu'allim al-thālith*) because of his role in establishing the "School of Isfahan".

In speaking about the "sources" of Mullā Ṣadrā, it must be remembered that all the ideas which Mullā Ṣadrā drew from these various sources served as construction blocks in a structure whose "style" is distinctly his own and indicative of a new intellectual perspective within the traditional Islamic world view. This truth will be borne out if one takes the trouble to make an actual comparison between the original "sources" and Ṣadr al-Dīn's use of them in his doctrinal expositions. It has been said that for example Mullā Ṣadrā took the doctrine of the unity and principiality of existence from the Sufis, the unity of the agent of intellection, the intellect and the intelligible from Abu'l-Ḥasan al-'Āmirī, and before him from Porphyry and certain aspects of his theory of knowledge from the *ishrāqīs.* But when an actual comparison is made between the original statements concerning these doctrines and their exposition by Mullā Ṣadrā, the transformation that these ideas have undergone in becoming elements in the intellectual universe of Ṣadr al-Dīn stands out clearly. Creativity in a traditional setting means not an individualistic discovery or creation of a "truth", but a fresh vision of that Reality which always is and will always be. But, being a new vision, it implies by definition a creative act in which the same universal truths receive a new interpretation and application in accordance with the particular moment in the historical unfolding of the tradition in question.

The illuminations Mullā Ṣadrā had received and the gnostic knowledge with which through his spiritual realization he was endowed acted as a philosopher's stone, they transmitted the substance of the elements received from previous Muslim saints, sages and philosophers and created his own vast synthesis. We may find in Mullā Ṣadrā's works, especially in the *Asfār,* multiple references to earlier Muslim sources, which make of this work a veritable encyclopedia of Islamic philosophy and metaphysics. We observe, however, in the parts of this *magnum opus* which deal with his own doctrines as well as in his other writings not merely outward adaptation and imitation but a total integration of earlier teachings into a new doctrinal exposition which has justly come to be known since then as the "Transcendent Theosophy" (*al-ḥikmat al-muta'āliyah*).

Notes

1. See for example M.T. Danechepazhuh's introduction to Mullā Ṣadrā's *Kasr al-aṣnām al-jāhiliyyah.* A few decades ago Ḍiā' al-Dīn Durrī tried to collect all the instances where Mullā Ṣadrā had cited earlier works without referring to the author and also spoke somewhat negatively of his having made use of so many sources without mentioning all of the authors and works involved. See his *Kanz al-ḥikmah,* vol. II, Tehran, 1316 (A.H. solar), pp. 157 ff. The actual collection of such instances made by Durrī has never (according to some of his acquaintances) been published or even seen in manuscript form.
2. See S.H. Nasr, *Three Muslim Sages,* p. 6.
3. No trace has been found of his personal library as yet but there is some hope that part of it at least may be found in the many private collections which still survive in Shiraz but which unfortunately are now being rapidly plundered.
4. There survive two copies of the *Asfār* in the Majlis Library in Tehran which illustrate this point. The first, MS. no. 106 in the *Fihrist-i Kitābkhāna-yi Majlis-i Shawrā-yi Millī,* bu Y. I'tiṣāmī, vol. II, Tehran, 1311 (A.H. solar), p. 53, contains very extensive glosses by Sayyid Abu'l-Ḥasan Jilwah, the famous Qajar *ḥakīm,* and in many instances where Mullā Ṣadrā writes "The *ḥakīm* has said . . . (*qāla'l-ḥakīm*)" he has identified who the *ḥakīm* was. He has also identified many unknown or little known works which were used by Mullā Ṣadrā. A second example is MS. no. 3980 of the same collection, again with glosses by Jilwah, on the *al-Jawāhir wa'l-a'rāḍ* (the second *safar* of the *Asfār*), which belonged to Mīrzā Ṭāhir Tunikābunī and which again reveals attempts on the part of Jilwah to identify some of the links between Mullā Ṣadrā and earlier Muslim sources.

5. These commentaries have unfortunately never received the scholarly study that they deserve.
6. Mullā Ṣadrā was also acquainted with the text of the Bible and quotes from both the Torah and the Gospels in his *Asfār*.
7. See S.H. Nasr, "*al-Ḥikmat al-ilāhiyyah* and *Kalām*", *Studia Islamica,* vol. XXXIV, 1971, pp. 139–49.
8. See H. Corbin (with the collaboration of S.H. Nasr and O. Yahya), *Histoire de la philosophie islamique,* vol. I, Paris, 1964, pp. 110ff.
9. On the influence of these sources on Mullā Ṣadrā see S.J. Sajjādī, "Ta'thīr-i Ikhwān-i Ṣafā' wa Ḥamīd al-Dīn Kirmānī dar Ṣadr al-Dīn Shīrāzī", *Revue de la Faculté des Lettres (Téhéran),* vol. IX, No. 3, 1341 (A.H. solar), pp. 89–96.
10. The relation between Mullā Ṣadrā and Ghazzālī bears special investigation. Although not studied extensively by the Shī'ite theologians and *ḥakīms*, Ghazzālī was nevertheless very well known to Mullā Ṣadrā. He may in fact be said to have known him more intimately than any of the other later Shī'ite intellectual figures except perhaps Mullā Muḥsin Fayḍ Kāshānī who wrote a Shī'ite version of the *Iḥyā'* entitled *Maḥajjat al-bayḍā' fī iḥyā' al-iḥyā'*. See the introduction by S.M. Mishkāt to the edition of this work, Tehran, 1380–1381 (A.H. lunar).
11. See S.H. Nasr, *Sufi Essays,* London, 1972, pp. 100–1.
12. See S.H. Nasr, *Islamic Studies,* p. 129. Mullā Ṣadrā's thinking on the Pre-Socratics can be best seen in his *Risālah fī ḥudūth al-'ālam,* in *Rasā'il,* pp. 67 ff.
13. See S.H. Nasr, *An Introduction to Islamic Cosmological Doctrines,* chapter 2.
14. See F. Jadaane, *L'influence du stoicisme sur la pensée musulmane,* Beirut, 1968; 'Uthmān Amīn, *al-Falsafat al-riwāqiyyah,* Cairo, 1959, and also his "Le stoicisme et la pensée musulmane", *La Revue Thomiste,* no. 1, t. LIX, 1959. Also H. Corbin, *Le livre des pénétrations métaphysiques,* pp. 165–6.
15. For example in the seventh *mash'ar* of his *Kitāb al-mashā'ir* he writes,

انا نقول: «ليس المجعول بالذات هو المسمّى بالماهية كما ذهب
اتباع الرواقيين، كالشيخ المقتول و من تبعه، و منهم العلاّمة
الدواني»

That is: "We affirm that that which is by essence the object of instauration (*maj'ūl*) is not what is called quiddity as has been professed by the *riwāqiyyūn* such as the martyred Shaykh [Suhrawardī] and those of his school, among whom is 'Allāmah Dawānī". See H. Corbin, *Le livre des pénétrations métaphysiques,* p 37 for the Arabic text and p. 157 for the French translation.
16. Like most other Muslim philosophers, Mullā Ṣadrā did not display interest in the other later schools of Graeco-Roman philosophy which were based on doubt and skepticism or which led to various forms of hedonism.
17. We have already dealt with the importance of the *Asfār* from this point of view in our *Islamic Studies,* chapter 11.
18. Mullā Ṣadrā's glosses (*Ta'līqah*) upon the *Shifā'* are among the most important ever written on this major *opus* of Islamic Peripatetic philosophy.
19. Mullā Ṣadrā also displays some knowledge of the *Qānūn,* especially its philosophical parts.
20. This important work dealing with diverse ontological questions has been at last edited by A. Badawi, Cairo, 1973. It is a key work for an understanding of Ibn Sīnā's views on existence (*wujūd*) and quiddity (*māhiyyah*).
21. Probably no major intellectual figure in later Islamic philosophy has been so completely neglected as Ghiyāth al-Dīn Manṣūr, whose writings, of which numerous manuscripts can be found in both Persia and India, deserve to be edited and carefully studied.

22. See S.H. Nasr, *Three Muslim Sages*, pp. 63–4, and S.H. Nasr "Suhrawardī" in M.M. Sharif (ed.), *A History of Muslim Philosophy*, vol. I, p. 380.
23. The names of Suhrawardī, Quṭb al-Dīn Shīrāzī and Mullā Ṣadrā have become bound together through the text, commentary (*sharḥ*) and glosses (*ta'līqāt*) upon the *Ḥikmat al-ishrāq*. The lithographed edition of the *Ḥikmat al-ishrāq*, which is a standard text for *ishrāqī* doctrines in traditional circles in Persia to this day, contains all three. But it must be added that, as was pointed out in the previous chapter, the glosses of Mullā Ṣadrā are not upon the commentary of Quṭb al-Dīn but upon the text of Suhrawardī itself. See H. Corbin, "Le thème de la résurrection chez Mollā Ṣadrā Shīrāzī (1050/1640) commentateur de Sohrawardī (587/1191)", in *Studies in Mysticism and Religion presented to Gershom G. Scholem*, Jerusalem, 1967, pp. 71–115.
24. The collected writings of this remarkable figure are being edited by S.J. Mūsawī Bihbahānī and S.I. Dībājī. See S.J. Mūsawī Bihbahānī, "Aḥwāl wa āthār-i Ṣā'in al-Dīn Turkah Iṣfahānī", *Collected Papers on Islamic Philosophy and Mysticism*, ed. by M. Mohaghegh and H. Landolt, McGill University, Institute of Islamic Studies, Tehran Branch, Tehran, 1971, pp. 99–135.

The Mullā Ṣadrā hall (tālār-i Mullā Ṣadrā) in the Khan school in Shiraz where the master taught for some thirty years

Chapter 5

What is the "Transcendent Theosophy"?

We have already noted that the term "Transcendent Theosophy" (*al-ḥikmat al-muta'āliyah*) was used by Sufis such as Qayṣarī long before Mullā Ṣadrā and should mention here that it even appears in the works of such masters of Peripatetic philosophy as Quṭb al-Dīn Shīrāzī.[1] But in these earlier instances the meaning attached to it was not by any means the same as that which we find in the writings of Mullā Ṣadrā and his students, who have given it a precise meaning and identified it with Ṣadr al-Dīn's new metaphysical and philosophical synthesis. It is, therefore, legitimate to delve here into the meaning and general characteristics of the "Transcendent Theosophy" and to prepare the ground for the analysis in a subsequent volume of the ideas and doctrines contained in its various branches.

The expression, *al-ḥikmat al-muta'āliyah,* comprises the two terms *al-ḥikmah* (meaning *theosophia*) and *muta'āliyah* (meaning exalted or transcendent). Although of course used by Mullā Ṣadrā, it became famous when Mullā Ṣadrā's students, both direct and indirect, used it to describe his school. Already a generation after Mullā Ṣadrā, 'Abd al-Razzāq Lāhījī, the master's son-in-law and one of his most illustrious students, called Mullā Ṣadrā's philosophy *al-ḥikmat al-muta'āliyah.*[2] By the Qajar period this usage had become so common that Sabziwārī in his famous *Sharḥ al-manẓūmah* did not even pause to explain the reason for using the term as the name for the school of the master whose doctrines he sought to elucidate in his own works.[3]

When we turn to the writings of Mullā Ṣadrā himself, we do not find any passages in which he explicitly designates his own school as *al-ḥikmat al-muta'āliyah.* The term as used by him is in fact related to the title of two of his works already cited in chapter 2, the major *opus, al-Ḥikmat al-muta'āliyah fī-l-asfār al-'aqliyyat al-arba'ah*, and one of the last or perhaps the very last work written by him entitled simply *al-Ḥikmat al-muta'āliyah.*[4] Even the use of the term *al-ḥikmat al-muta'āliyah* in *al-Shawāhid al-rubūbiyyah*[5] is with reference to this latter book of Mullā Ṣadra rather than to his school of thought. The fact that the term *al-ḥikmat al-muta'āliyah* came to be identified with Mullā Ṣadrā's doctrines by his students and by the public at large was most likely due to two factors: one, the title of the *Asfār,* in which is implied the existence of a school and the world view delineated by the metaphysical doctrines, contained in this book in whose matrix (*fī*) the four intellectual journeys toward the stations of certainty are made; and two, the likely presence of oral teaching by the master himself according to which *al-ḥikmat al-muta'āliyah* was meant to be not only the title of some of his writings but also the name of his whole school. Although this latter point cannot by definition be substantiated through written documents, its confirmation by all the leading traditional masters of this school in Persia today, masters who have all received the oral tradition complementing the written text through a chain of teachers reaching back to Mullā Ṣadrā himself, is the strongest argument for its acceptance.

Be that as it may, the term *al-ḥikmat al-muta'āliyah* has come to mean the particular school of traditional theosophy formulated by Mullā Ṣadrā, a designation that began in his own day and has continued to the present. It is a most appropriate name for his school, not only for historical reasons, but also because the doctrines of Mullā Ṣadrā are veritably both *ḥikmah* or theosophy in its original sense and an intellectual vision of the transcendent (the *muta'āliyah*) which leads to the Transcendent Itself. The school of Mullā Ṣadrā is therefore "Transcendent Theosophy" both for historical and metaphysical reasons.

In trying to understand how Mullā Ṣadrā defined the "Transcendent Theosophy", we must turn to his own definitions of theosophy (*al-ḥikmah*) or philosophy (*al-falsafah*). 'When he speaks of *al-ḥikmah* he is in fact speaking of the "Transcendent Theosophy", because for him true *ḥikmah* is *al-ḥikmat al-muta'āliyah* which he expounded. It is of interest to note that like earlier Islamic philosophers, and even more than them, Mullā Ṣadrā was intensely interested in the definition and meaning of *falsafah* and *ḥikmah*. He discussed them in several of his works and defined them more than once, drawing for his definition on earlier sources and synthesizing various views in his own characteristic fashion. In one of his famous definitions, he considers *ḥikmah* as the vehicle through which "man becomes an intelligible world resembling the objective world and similar to the order of universal existence".[7] In a more extensive definition of *falsafah* in the *Asfār*, he echoes views all the way from Plato to Suhrawardī, stating, "*Falsafah* is the perfecting of the human soul to the extent of human possibility through knowledge of the essential realities of things as they are in themselves and through judgment concerning their existence established upon demonstration[8] and not derived from opinion or through imitation. Or if thou likest thou canst say, it is to give intelligible order to the world to the extent of human possibility in order to gain 'resemblance' to the Divine".[9] One of the foremost expositors of the school of Mullā Ṣadrā during the last century, Mīrzā Mahdī Āshtiyānī,[10] has distinguished the "Transcendent Theosophy" from earlier schools of philosophy in the following pertinent comment: "It [*al-ḥikmat al-muta'āliyah*] entails the unity of being [*tawḥīd al-wujūd*] in contrast to Peripatetic philosophy, in which is to be found only the unity of necessity [i.e., Necessary Being] (*tawḥīd wujūb wājib* [*al-wujūd*]), not the unity of being".[11]

If the definitions of *ḥikmah* given by Mullā Ṣadrā are analyzed along with the pertinent postscript of Āshtiyānī, it will be discovered that the concept of *ḥikmah* which in fact is none other than *al-ḥikmat al-muta 'āliyah,* is identified with a wisdom or theosophy which is based on a purely metaphysical foundation reached through intellectual intuition and at the same time presented in a rational but not rationalistic form and making use of rational arguments. They also show that this theosophy is related to realization, to the transformation of the being of the recipient of this knowledge. Furthermore, as we delve more fully into the writings of Mullā Sadrā, we discover that the methods proposed for the realization of this knowledge are related to religion and cannot become accessible except by means of revelation.

There are, therefore, as already stated, three basic principles upon which the "Transcendent Theosophy" stands: intellectual intuition or illumination (*kashf* or *dhawq* or *ishrāq*); reason and rational demonstration (*'aql* or *istidlāl*); and religion or revelation (*shar'*, or *waḥy*). It is by combining the knowledge derived from these sources that the synthesis of Mullā Ṣadrā was brought about. This synthesis aimed to harmonize the knowledge that is accessible to man through the following means, namely, Sufism, the school of *ishrāq*, rational philosophy (identified by Mullā Ṣadrā with the Peripatetic school) and the religious sciences including theology (*kalām*). The characteristics of the "Transcendent Theosophy" become more clear if it is compared with each of these branches of the traditional Islamic sciences.[13]

In the discussion in Chapter 4 of the sources of Mullā Ṣadrā's doctrines, we showed how closely his teachings were related to those of the Sufis, particularly to Ibn 'Arabī, Ṣadr al-Dīn al-Qunyawī, 'Abd al-Razzāq Kāshānī, Dā'ūd al-Qayṣarī and other masters of Ibn 'Arabī's school. If his teachings were to be compared and contrasted with theirs, it could be said that the Sufi metaphysics of these masters is the intellectualized version of their spiritual vision. In the case of Ibn 'Arabī especially, this metaphysics presents itself as so many strokes of lightning, each of which illuminates an aspect of the landscape of ultimate Reality. These flashes of light are transformed by Mullā Ṣadrā – and also to a certain extent by such figures as Qayṣarī before him – into a more steady and continuous light. Ṣadr al-Dīn seeks to present a more systematic metaphysical exposition, to provide logical proofs and to explain aspects which the earlier Sufi masters had passed over in silence or simply stated in brief form as a gift of heaven and the result of their spiritual visions. There are no major points in which Mullā Ṣadrā opposes the teachings of Ibn 'Arabī as he opposes certain theses of the Peripatetics and the Illuminationists, except perhaps in the question of evil, and in the question of free-will and predestination, which he treats somewhat differently from Ibn 'Arabī. But he does discuss many points which are not touched upon by Ibn 'Arabī and his school but are implied by them. In a sense Mullā Ṣadrā provides both a more logical and systematic basis for the Sufi metaphysics of the school of Ibn 'Arabī and a commentary upon and extension of his works. In fact, besides being one of the leading philosophers and theosophers of Islam, Mullā Ṣadrā must also be considered one of the foremost commentators on Ibn 'Arabī and his students.

If we compare the "Transcendent Theosophy" with the "Theosophy of the Orient of Light" (*al-ḥikmat al-ishrāq*) of

Suhrawardī, we would find both a close rapport, already alluded to earlier, and certain differences which would aid our understanding of the "Transcendent Theosophy" itself. It could be said that Mullā Ṣadrā realized more fully in his own being the ideal of the theosopher (*muta'allih*) which Suhrawardī announced and strove to realize.[14] He succeeded more fully than Suhrawardī in providing a rational foundation for the knowledge that issues from spiritual vision. In this endeavour he owes much to Suhrawardī, who was the first to take a step in this direction; but Mullā Ṣadrā followed this direction to its end and was able to deal with more questions than Suhrawardī and to explore some of them in greater depth.

Similarly, the attitude of the two men toward Ibn Sīnā and Peripatetic philosophy is not exactly the same. Although Suhrawardī knew Ibn Sīnā well and wrote several important works such as the *Talwīḥāt* and the *Muṭāraḥāt*, which are in reality re-formulations of Ibn Sīnā's teachings, he criticized Ibn Sīnā openly in both the *Qiṣṣat al-ghurbat al-gharbiyyah*[15] and the *Ḥikmat al-ishrāq*.[16] Mullā Ṣadrā, however, while also a critic of many points of Peripatetic philosophy, as we shall demonstrate shortly, was one of Ibn Sīnā's chief commentators and was able to integrate his teachings into the "Transcendent Theosophy" more fully than Suhrawardī was able to harmonize Peripatetic philosophy with *ḥikmat al-ishrāq*. Whereas for Suhrawardī Peripatetic philosophy was a necessary basis for a study of *ishrāqī* theosophy, for Mullā Ṣadrā it was an element that was integrated in an organic fashion into the very texture of the "Transcendent Theosophy".

As far as the strictly speaking religious sources are concerned, there is also a distinction between what we find in the "Transcendent Theosophy" and in *ishrāqī* theosophy. Again the credit must go to Suhrawardī for being the first Islamic philosopher to quote Quranic verses in his philosophical works and to seek to harmonize the meaning of the revealed verses with the tenets of theosophy. But once again it was Mullā Ṣadrā who followed this approach through and succeeded in interweaving the texts of the Holy Quran and *Ḥadīth* with his own theosophical exposition in a manner that was unprecedented. There is also this difference, that Suhrawardī made use of Quranic verses and the sayings of the Prophet, while Mullā Ṣadrā had recourse to the sayings of the Shi'ite Imams, such as the *Nahj al-balāghah* of 'Alī and the traditions assembled in

Kulaynī's *Uṣūl al-kāfī*, in addition to the Quran and prophetic *Ḥadīth*. Moreover, Mullā Ṣadrā must be considered a major Quranic commentator in his own right, ranking with the foremost commentators in Islamic history, a unique distinction among Islamic philosophers.

When we come to more particular points of difference between Mullā Ṣadrā and Suhrawardī, we realize that, although closely related, the "Transcendent Theosophy" departs on many points from *ishrāqī* theosophy, of which some of the most basic will be mentioned. The most important difference is of course Mullā Ṣadrā's assertion of the principiality of existence (*aṣālat al-wujūd*) in contrast to the principiality of quiddity (*aṣālat al-māhiyyah*) held by Suhrawardī, a difference which Corbin has called the basis of the "revolution" brought about by Mullā Ṣadrā in Islamic philosophy.[17] This difference leads in turn to a difference in view concerning the question of change and transformation, the gradation of beings, eschatology, etc., which a close comparison of Mullā Ṣadrā's teachings with those of Suhrawardī reveals.[18]

Another distinct difference between Mullā Ṣadrā and Suhrawardī concerns the world of imagination (*'ālam al-khayāl*) with which we hope to deal fully in the subsequent volume. Here suffice it to say that Suhrawardī was the first Islamic philosopher to assert that this faculty within the human soul was independent of the body (*tajarrud*), and hence that it continued to exist after corporeal death. But he did not assert the existence of the objective and cosmic counterpart of this microcosmic imagination, whereas Mullā Ṣadrā believes in a macrocosmic world of imagination (*khayāl al-munfaṣil*) as well as a microcosmic one (*khayāl al-muttaṣil*) with profound consequences for problems of the posthumous becoming of man and eschatology in general.

Finally, in his natural philosophy Mullā Ṣadrā departs from the views of Suhrawardī to return to the hylomorphism of Ibn Sīnā, but interprets this doctrine in the light of the principle of substantial motion (*al-ḥarakat al-jawhariyyah*) which is one of the basic features of the "Transcendent Theosophy". This principle leads Mullā Ṣadrā to an interpretation of many aspects of natural philosophy and also eschatology that is different from *ishrāqī* theosophy, although here as in other domains the debt which Mullā Ṣadrā owes to Suhrawardī is clear. The most cursory study of the doctrines of the two masters will reveal that

Mullā Ṣadrā could not have appeared had there not been a Suhrawardī to prepare the ground for him. Also, as in the case of Ibn 'Arabī, so with Suhrawardī – Mullā Ṣadrā must be considered among the latter's most important interpreters and commentators. In fact along with Muḥammad Shahrazūrī and Quṭb al-Dīn Shīrāzī, Mullā Ṣadrā is the most outstanding commentator and expositor of the *ishrāqī* school, a commentator who, while commenting upon the works of the master of *ishrāq*, developed *ishrāqī* theosophy in a particular direction and made it a cornerstone for his own "Transcendent Theosophy".

When we turn to Ibn Sīnā and Peripatetic philosophy, we see again that the "Transcendent Theosophy" of Mullā Ṣadrā owes a great deal to the *mashshā'ī* school and especially to Ibn Sīnā himself, but that it departs from this school on certain basic points. Mullā Ṣadrā was himself a master of Peripatetic thought and his *Sharḥ al-hidāyah*, which is an exposition of Peripatetic philosophy, has served for centuries as a text for students of Ibn Sīnā's school of thought in the eastern land of Islam.[19] Moreover, Mullā Ṣadrā is among the most precise and profound commentators of Ibn Sīnā himself, his *Glosses* (*Ḥāshiyah*) upon the *Shifā'* being perhaps the best ever written on the metaphysical sections of this monumental work. Despite the profound debt of the "Transcendent Theosophy" to the *mashahā'ī* school, however, there are basic points of difference, some of the most important of which are mentioned here.[20]

The fundamental difference between the doctrines of Mullā Ṣadrā and Ibn Sīnā can be traced back to the different ways in which they treat ontology. Mullā Ṣadrā conceives of being as a graded reality which remains one despite its gradation, while Ibn Sīnā, although conceding the principiality of existence in each existent, believes the existence of each existent to be different from that of other existents. Moreover, Ibn Sīnā conceives of becoming as an external process which affects solely the accidents of things; hence he denies transsubstantial motion (*al-ḥarakat al-jawhariyyah*), which forms a cornerstone of the "Transcendent Theosophy". The "inquietude of existence" as Corbin has described Mullā Ṣadrā's doctrine is absent from Ibn Sīnā's vision of the Universe.

The denial of transsubstantial motion as well as of the gradation of being led Ibn Sīnā to the denial of the Platonic "ideas" and the horizontal and vertical hierarchy of archetypes and intelligences which form such an important part of the teachings of both Suhrawardī and Mullā Ṣadrā. Likewise, Ibn Sīnā denies the possibility of the union between the intellect and the intelligible (*ittiḥād al-ʿāqil wa'l-maʿqūl*) again because of his denial of the possibility of transsubstantial motion.

Mullā Ṣadrā believes that love (*al-ʿishq*) is a principle that runs through the arteries of the Universe and exists at all levels of existence. This esoteric doctrine is not absent from Ibn Sīnā's writings, as we see in his famous *Risālah fi'l-ʿishq* (*Treatise on Love*),[21] but nowhere does Ibn Sīnā provide full demonstration for this principle or integrate it organically into his metaphysics.

The denial of the principle of substantial motion by Ibn Sīnā and its assertion by Mullā Ṣadrā has also led the two masters to treat completely differently the problems of the "eternity" of the heavens and the *hylé,* the whole problem of the "newness" or "eternity" of the world as well as the question of the manner in which plants and animals grow. It has led to a whole series of differences between them in questions pertaining to cosmology and natural philosophy.

Likewise in psychology, there are basic differences perhaps more evident than in all other branches of traditional philosophy. Ibn Sīnā deals with psychology as a branch of natural philosophy (*ṭabīʿiyyāt*) and is concerned mostly with the description of the faculties of the soul. Mullā Ṣadrā, on the contrary, deals with psychology as a branch of metaphysics (*ilāhiyyāt*) and deals extensively in a manner that is unparalleled in Islamic philosophy with the origin, growth, posthumous becoming and final entelechy of the soul. There are even differences between the two concerning the very faculties of the soul and the manner in which the soul is related to the external and internal faculties.

The features which distinguish the "Transcendent Theosophy" from the religious sciences and *kalām* are the most obvious and clear of all. In the field of the religious sciences the "Transcendent Theosophy" accepts them fully and reasserts their teachings but seeks always to elucidate their inner meaning. For example, in his Quranic commentaries which form a basic part of the "Transcendent Theosophy", Mullā Ṣadrā reasserts all the principles of *tafsīr* of the earlier commentators, to which he adds his hermeneutic and esoteric interpretation (*ta'wīl*). In the field of jurisprudence (*fiqh*) and the study of the Divine Law (*Sharīʿah*), although Mullā Ṣadrā did not write an independent work on these subjects, in his frequent references he always aims to bring out their inner meaning. This is particularly true in the case of the rites of Islam (*'ibādāt*), in which Mullā Ṣadrā, followed by many of his students, direct and indirect, from Mullā Muḥsin Fayḍ Kāshānī and Qāḍī Sa'īd Qummī to Ḥājjī Mullā Hādī Sabziwārī, tries to expound the esoteric meaning of daily Islamic ritual practices and injunctions under the heading of a subject that has become known as "the mysteries of worship" (*asrār al-'ibābāt*). One of the distinguishing features of the "Transcendent Theosophy" is that, in contrast to earlier Islamic philosophy but like Sufism,[22] it is concerned with the inner meaning of concrete and detailed acts of Islamic worship, whereas the earlier Islamic philosophers like Ibn Sīnā dealt with the meaning of worship in a more general manner.[23]

When dealing with *kalām,* Mullā Ṣadrā and all of his followers, while knowledgeable in its science, were opposed to its methods and approaches.[24] The "Transcendent Theosophy" resembles *kalām* in the sense that it takes into consideration all the problems with which *kalām* is concerned, whereas some of the theological and religious problems of *kalām* were not considered by earlier Islamic philosophers. But Mullā Ṣadrā and his students consider the *mutakallimūn* not competent to solve many of the problems to which they address themselves. They are especially opposed to the "voluntarism" of the *mutakallimūn* which is such a salient feature of the Ash'arite school. The "Transcendent Theosophy" solves the problems discussed in *kalām* in a manner which is properly speaking metaphysical rather than theological and which differs widely from the methods of *kalām.*

In conclusion we can summarize by ṣaying that the "Transcendent Theosophy" is a new perspective in Islamic intellectual life based on the synthesis and harmonization of nearly all the earlier schools of Islamic thought. It is also a school in which the tenets of revelation, the verities received through spiritual vision and illumination and the rigorous demands of logic and rational demonstration are harmonized into a unity. It is a doctrine which can be fully understood only in reference to the thought of the schools which preceded it. Yet it has its own distinct features including its separation of metaphysics and psychology from natural philosophy[25] and the establishment of a clear distinction between general metaphysics (*al-umūr al-'āmmah*) and theodicy (*al-umūr al-khāṣṣah*). These features also concern fundamental aspects of the metaphysical content of the "Transcendent Theosophy" with which we hope to deal in the complementary volume to follow soon. In the "Transcendent Theosophy", as in every authentic traditional school of thought, we find the same metaphysical truths that have always been and will always be but expressed in a formulation that is new because it issues from a new vision of the Real. We also see in the birth-process of this school the application of the perennial truths through veritable creativity to new needs and conditions at a particular moment in the life of a living tradition. This process caused the genesis of a school which is at once new and continuous with the tradition from which it issued. The "Transcendent Theosophy" is a new branch of the tree of Islamic intellectuality intended to provide for the intellectual needs of a particular part of the Islamic community at a certain moment of time and period of history which continues to our own day. It came into being in order to guarantee the continuation of the intellectual life of the tradition in the new cycle of its historical existence and to be one more expression late in human history of that philosophy or wisdom which is at once perennial and universal, the *sophia perennis* which the Islamic sages have referred to as *al-ḥikmat al-khālidah* or, in its Persian version, as *jāwīdān khirad*.

wa'Llāh^u a'lam

Notes

1. In his *Sharḥ al-hidāyah*, Tehran, 1313 (A.H. lunar), p. 195, Mullā Ṣadrā quotes from Quṭb al-Dīn's commentary upon the *Canon* of Ibn Sīnā as follows to show that Ibn Sīnā was well-grounded in the "Transcendent Theosophy"

«ان الشيخ و لاغيره من الحكماء الراسخين فى الحكمة المتعالية ذهبوا و اعتقدوا ان المدرك للمحسوسات الجزئيه هو الحواس الخمس».

Quṭb al-Dīn also refers to the "Transcendent Theosophy" in his *Durrat al-tāj*. The research of S.J. Ashtiyānī conveyed to us in a letter confirms the view that before Mullā Ṣadrā "Transcendent Theosophy" meant the *ḥikmat-i ilāhī* of the *veritable* philosophers and as such was widely used. To quote Āshtiyānī's phrase:

«حکمت متعالیه که همان حکمت الهی روش اهل تحقیق باشد در همه‌جا قبل از ملاصدرا به چشم می‌خورد.»

Among Mullā Ṣadrā's contemporaries the outstanding *ḥakīm*, Mullā Shamsā Gīlānī, who in fact opposed Mullā Ṣadrā's doctrines in many ways, also wrote a work entitled *al-Ḥikmat al-muta'āliyah*.

2. "There are numerous witnesses to the exaltation of his power in the sacred stations of spiritual vision and countless works and 'books' (*asfār*) which are the messengers of his thought concerning the *ḥikmat-i muta'āliyah*". See J. Muṣliḥ, *Falsafa-yi 'ālī*, vol. I, *Risāla-yi wujūd*, Tehran, 1377 (A.H. lunar), p. yk, where the letter of Lāhījī to Mullā Ṣadrā is reproduced.
3. In his own commentary upon the eighth verse of the metaphysics of the *Sharḥ al-manẓūmah*, Sabziwārī interprets the verse:

(لاقت برسم بمداد النور)

as

«لاقت ای الحکمة المتعالیة و المنظومة باعتبار اشتمالها علی مسائل الحکمة المتعالیة...»

See Sabziwārī, *Sharḥ-i ghurar al-farā'id* or *Sharḥ-i manẓūmah*, ed. by M. Mohaghegh and T. Izutsu, Part I, Tehran, 1969, p. 39 of the Arabic commentary upon the verses.

4. See the Persian introduction to this book by S.J. Āshtiyānī in his edition of this work; also the English preface by S.H. Nasr.
5. Concerning the soul's knowledge of universals Mullā Ṣadrā writes, "We have dealt with this extensively in *al-Asfār al-arba'ah* and in an intermediate fashion in *al-Ḥikmat al-muta'āliyah*". See *al-Shawāhid al-rubūbiyyah*, ed. by S.J. Āshtiyānī, p. 34.
6. For Mullā Ṣadrā as for the other Islamic philosophers of the later period in Persia, *ḥikmah* and *falsafah* are used almost synonymously in contrast to the earlier periods of Islamic philosophy when many philosophers and theologians such as Fakhr al-Dīn al-Rāzī sought to distinguish between them. See S.H. Nasr, *An Introduction to Islamic Cosmological Doctrines*, prologue.
7.

«و صیرورتها عالما عقلیا مضاهیاً للعالم العینی و مشابهاً لنظام الوجود»

See the introduction of S.A. Āshtiyānī to Ṣadr al-Dīn Shīrāzī, *al-Shawāhid al-rubūbiyyah*, p. 7.

Concerning this and other definitions of *Ḥikmah* and *falsafah* by Mullā Ṣadrā and other Islamic philosophers see S.H. Nasr, "The Meaning and Role of Philosophy in Islam", *Studia Islamica*, XXXVII, 1973, pp. 57–80; see also S.H. Nasr, *The Tradition of Islamic Philosophy in Persia* (forthcoming).

8. As we have had occasion to mention already in our other writings, *burhān* as understood in Islamic philosophy is not exactly demonstration as currently understood in the parlance of logic in the West. There is an element of intellectual certainty and illumination of the mind connected with *burhān* which is lacking in the term "demonstration" by which is it usually translated.

9.

«ان الفلسفة استكمال النفس الانسانية بمعرفة حقائق الموجودات على ما هى عليها والحكم بوجودها تحقيقا بالبراهين لا اخذا بالظن والتقليد، بقدر الوسع الانساني، و ان شئت قلت نظم العالم نظما عقليا على حسب الطاقة البشرية لتحصيل التشبه بالبارئ تعالى».

Al-Ḥikmat al-muta'āliyah fi'l-asfār al-arba'ah, vol. I, part 1, Tehran, 1387 (A.H.), p. 20.

10. Concerning this figure see the English introduction of T. Izutsu to M. Āshtiyānī, *Commentary on Sabzawārī's Sharḥ-i manẓūmah,* Tehran, 1973.

11.

«وهى المشتملة على توحيد الوجود بخلاف حكمة المشّاء فانّ فيها توحيد الواجب فقط لاتوحيد الوجود».

Comments made by Mīrzā Mahdī in his teaching of the commentary of Qayṣarī upon the *Fuṣūṣ* of Ibn 'Arabī and recorded by Professor J. Falāṭūrī as *Taqrīrāt* written in the margin of a copy of the lithographed edition of the Qayṣarī commentary (p. 16, second column, line 2) now in the possession of Professor Falāṭūrī. We are grateful to Professor Falāṭūrī for making this very pertinent commentary of Mīrzā Mahdī upon the term *al-ḥikmat al-muta'āliyah* in this work available to us.

12. In his introduction to the *Asfār* as well as in numerous instances in the *Sih aṣl* and *Kasr aṣnām al-jāhiliyyah,* Mullā Ṣadrā refers to *al-riyāḍāt al-shar'iyyah* (ascetic practices derived from the *Sharī'ah*)and the spiritual discipline learned from the saints (*awliyā'*) and going back to the Prophet. He makes clear the necessity of possessing religious faith (*īmān*) and of practicing the spiritual disciplines contained within the Islamic revelation in order to be able to gain access to the *ḥikmah* which is for him a divine science, a *scientia sacra,* hidden within both revelation and substance of the human soul.

13. Sufism in its theoretical aspect is a "science" in the traditional sense of *scientia sacra,* while in its practical aspect it is connected to a way of living and being and thus is related to the pole of existence rather than knowledge and cannot, strictly speaking, be categorized as a science.

14. On Suhrawardī's description of the *muta'allih* see his *Ḥikmat al-ishrāq,* ed. by H. Corbin, in *Oeuvres philosophiques et mystiques,* vol. I, Tehran-Paris, 1952, and 1977, p. 12.

It is with this definition in mind that the title of *Ṣadr al-muta'allihīn* was bestowed upon Mullā Ṣadrā. It can therefore be said that indirectly the title by which Mullā Ṣadrā is commonly known in traditional circles in Persia to this day was bestowed upon him by Suhrawardī who opened the path towards the possibility of the appearance of a Mullā Ṣadrā.

15. See Suhrawardī, *Oeuvres philosophiques et mystiques,* vol. I, pp. 275–76.

16. The whole of the third chapter, *al-maqālat al-thālithah,* criticizing the Peripatetics is addressed most of all to the teachings of Ibn Sīnā and his school.

17. See Corbin's introduction of Mullā Ṣadrā's *al-Mashā'ir, Le Livre des pénétrations métaphysiques.* We have already asserted in our previous writings that if light is interpreted to mean existence in Suhrawardī, then he also can be said to accept the "principiality of existence" because for him the reality of all things is in the light which forms their very substance. Nevertheless, there is no doubt

that the ontological doctrines of Suhrawardī and Mullā Ṣadrā are different because of this difference of interpretation between them. See S.H. Nasr, *Three Muslim Sages*, pp. 69–70; and Nasr, "Suhrawardī", in M.M. Sharif (ed.), *A History of Muslim Philosophy*, vol. I, pp. 385 on.

18. Our goal here is not to make such a detailed comparison but to bring out the salient features of the "Transcendent Theosophy" by comparing it with already existing schools of Islamic thought. As various schools of Islamic philosophy become better known, it will soon become necessary for scholars to make careful comparative studies of different schools of Islamic philosophy itself as well as of Islamic philosophy and other schools of traditional philosophy in both East and West. See S.H. Nasr, "Condition for meaningful comparative philosophy", *Philosophy East and West*, vol. 22, no. 1, Jan. 1972, pp. 53–61; see also Nasr, *Islam and the Plight of Modern Man*, London, 1976, chs. 3 and 4.
19. In the Indian subcontinent and Afghanistan, in fact, the *Sharḥ al-hidāyah* of Mullā Ṣadrā, which is a veritable masterpiece as a summary of Peripatetic philosophy, has been the most popular text of Islamic philosophy since the 11th/17th century being taught more widely than the works of Ibn Sīnā himself.
20. Concerning the differences between Mullā Ṣadrā and Ibn Sīnā, see the introduction of S.J. Āshtiyānī to *Sih risālah az Ṣadr al-Dīn Shīrāzī*, introduction, pp. 31 ff.
21. See E.L. Fackenheim, "A Treatise on Love by Ibn Sīnā", *Medieval Studies*, vol. 7, 1945, pp. 208–28.
22. Many Sufis such as Ghazzālī, Ibn 'Arabī and in recent times Shaykh al-'Alawī have written specific treatises on the esoteric meaning of Islamic rites such as the daily prayers, fasting or pilgrimage. The "Transcendent Theosophy" follows the Sufi tradition in this respect.
23. For example, Ibn Sīnā in his treatise on pilgrimage to the tombs of saints discusses the importance of visiting sanctuaries and the inner effect it has upon the human soul while Qāḍī Sa'īd Qummī in his *Asrār al-'ibādāt*, ed. by S.M.B. Sabziwārī, Tehran, 1339 (A.H. solar) (studied in part in H. Corbin, "Configuration du Temple de la Ka'ba comme sécret de la vie spirituelle", *Eranos-Jahrbuch*, 1967, pp. 79–166) delves into the esoteric meaning of concrete acts and words which form a part of the pilgrimage performed by Muslims at Mecca and promulgated by Islamic religious law.
24. See S.H. Nasr, "*al-Ḥikmat al-ilāhiyyah* and *Kalām*", *Studia Islamica*, vol. XXXIV, 1971, pp. 139–149.
25. The separation brought about by Mullā Ṣadrā between metaphysics and psychology on the one hand and natural philosophy on the other does not concern only the manner in which these subjects are treated. Rather, it is related to the way in which Mullā Ṣadrā deals with metaphysics and psychology without relying upon natural philosophy or basing his arguments upon elements drawn from physics.

Chapter 6

The Metaphysics of Ṣadr al-Dīn Shīrāzī and its Influence on Islamic Philosophy in Qajar Persia

Despite the flood of literature in recent years on Qajar Persia and its religious and even intellectual history, little systematic study has been carried out in European languages on the very active tradition of Islamic Philosophy during this era which is closely tied to the more manifest religious and social movements of the period.[1] While most scholars of this era simply ignore this tradition as if it did not exist, a few who have read a work or two on the later tradition of Islamic philosophy believe that because of the predominance of the teachings of Ṣadr al-Dīn Shīrāzī, Islamic philosophy during the Qajar period was simply a continuation or repetition of his teachings. In reality, however, the Islamic philosophy of this period, far from being homogeneous, displayed a rich variety ranging from those who defended Avicennan metaphysics to the Shaykhīs who rejected all the schools of *ḥikmat-i ilāhī* in the name of their own *ḥikmat* based only on the teachings of the Shi'ite Imams. Even Sabziwārī, the most illustrious defender of Mullā Ṣadrā during this period, had to defend Ṣadrian metaphysics constantly against its opponents.[2]

Yet there is no doubt that the metaphysical teachings of Ṣadr al-Dīn were central to the intellectual life of Qajar Persia and were of great importance not only for those who considered themselves as his followers, but even by those who opposed him, as is seen in the writings of Shaykh Aḥmad Aḥsā'ī, the founder of the Shaykhī movement and Sayyid Muḥammad the Bāb, founder of Bābism. To understand the main current of religious philosophy during this period, it is necessary to comprehend the central tenets of the incomparable metaphysical edifice of Mullā

Ṣadrā, along with its influence among both those who accepted it fervently or partially and those who opposed it for one reason or another.

Many of the traditional masters of Islamic philosophy in Persia to this day consider Mullā Ṣadrā as the foremost among Islamic metaphysicians, and indeed this view has been expressed by numerous authorities since the writings of Mullā Ṣadrā first became disseminated in the Safavid period. It would not be an exaggeration to say that within the annals of Islamic philosophy no single figure has dealt with metaphysics in such a detailed, systematic and at the same time profound manner.[3] Compared to Ibn Sīnā, Mullā Ṣadrā's treatment of *ilāhiyyāt* is at once more inward and gnostic and more extensive, although Ibn Sīnā's treatment of *ṭabī'iyyāt* is more complete than that of Mullā Ṣadrā. And compared to Ibn 'Arabī, Mullā Ṣadrā's exposition of metaphysics is more systematic and 'continuous', in many instances incorporating those 'discontinuous' flashes of inspiration, which characterise the gnostic doctrines of the master from Murcia, into a closely woven pattern.

Mullā Ṣadrā, in his metaphysics, is concerned essentially with Being, although he was fully aware of the supra-ontological nature of the Supreme Principle and its state above all limitations, including even the condition of standing above limitations. His discussion of the Absolute in its completely undetermined and supra-ontological aspect reveals the completeness of his metaphysical doctrines, which do not remain bound to the ontological level in the Aristotelian sense, even while making use of the language of ontology. When Mullā Ṣadrā speaks of Absolute Being as the 'Hidden Ipseity' (*al-huwiyyat al-ghaybiyyah*) transcending all limitations, he is in fact speaking of the supreme Principle in its completely unmanifested state, even above the ontological principle which is its first determination. Yet he uses the term *wujūd* in connection with it, so that at a superficial glance it might seem that he is not discussing anything above ontology. In actuality, however, the metaphysics of Mullā Ṣadrā begins with the Absolute Principle which transcends all limitations, then leads to Being which is its first determination and the creative Principle, and finally concerns itself with existence, in both its universal and particular aspects.[4]

To understand the metaphysics of Mullā Ṣadrā, it is necessary to be thoroughly familiar with Islamic philosophy before him. Only then can one understand the transformation that was brought about by Mullā Ṣadrā in this philosophy.[5] The earlier Islamic philosophers, especially of the Peripatetic school, were concerned with existents, *mawjūd* (*ens,* or *das Seiendes*) following Ardistotle, who defined metaphysics as the science of the 'existent *qua* existent' (*to on he on*). Although later Islamic philosophers interpret *mawjūd* and *wujūd* to be the same, [6] there is no doubt that Fārābian and Avicennan ontology was concerned primarily with *mawjūd.* It was in fact this interpretation of metaphysics that the West adopted from Islamic sources and which remained alive in Western philosophy until modern times. For Mullā Ṣadrā, however, the proper subject of metaphysics is the very act of being, *wujūd (esse, actus essendi or das Sein*).[7] Long before M. Heidegger pointed out the difference between *das Sein* and *das Seiende,* Mullā Ṣadrā had elevated true metaphysics to the level of the study of the very act of being , that mysterious *fiat lux* which causes things to leave the ocean of non-existence and become endowed with the gift of existence[8]. For Mullā Ṣadrā, metaphysics must be concerned not with things that exist, or existents, but with the very act of existence which is a ray cast from Pure Being Itself in the direction of nothingness.[9] Through this major transformation Mullā Ṣadrā resuscitated Islamic philosophy and made of it a bridge between exoteric religion and pure esotericism, of which in fact his theosophy is a particular version.

The metaphysics of Mullā Ṣadrā is based, like that of other Islamic philosophers and going back to al-Kindī and al-Fārābī, upon the distinction between existence (*wujūd*) and quiddity (*māhiyyah*) or essence.[10] This distinction is one of the most profound in metaphysics and stands along with such distinctions as principle and manifestation, essence and form, substance and accident, etc., as basic to an exposition in human language of the nature of Reality in its source and various levels of manifestation. It is in fact so deeply ingrained in the structure of Islamic philosophy that no school has left it out of its consideration and doctrinal language. It has also left its indelible mark upon Latin scholasticism where the very term quiddity (from *quid est* in Latin) is a literal translation of *māhiyyah.*[11]

In traditional courses on Islamic philosophy, long sessions are usually devoted to infusing the mind of the student with the habit of being able to distinguish clearly between existence and quiddity, and only after these two concepts are clear in his mind is he allowed to proceed with the study of the general principles of metaphysics (*al-umūr al-'āmmah*). In the works of Mullā Ṣadrā, however, usually the discussion of existence comes at the beginning-with only a reference to the distinction between existence and quiddity–and only after elucidating the 'principles concerning quiddity' (*aḥkām al–māhiyyah*).[12]

The order in which Mullā Ṣadrā sets out to expound the 'principles' of existence and quiddity can be best understood by turning to the contents of the first *safar* of the *Asfār* in which his most extensive discussion of ontology is to be found, with a more condensed version of the ideas appearing in some of his other works such as *al-Shawāhid al-rubūbiyyah* and *al-Mashā'ir*.

In his *magnum opus*, the *Asfār*, the first three stages (*marāḥil*) of the first *safar* deal with *wujūd*, the fourth with *māhiyyah*, and the fifth once again with *wujūd* in the light of the relation between the one and the many.

The first three stages, which contain the heart of Mullā Ṣadrā's metaphysics, proceed in the following order:

The first stage (*marḥalah*).

The first 'way' (*minhāj*)

Chapter (*faṣl*) one: That *wujūd* is the subject of metaphysics.

Chapter two: That the concept of existence is shared in meaning by various existents.

Chapter three: That the concept of existence is not among the constituent differentia of individual existents.

Chapter four: On the principiality of existence.

Chapter five: On what is the cause of the individuation of existence.

Chapter six : That ontological realities are simple entities.

Chapter seven: That the reality of existence has no cause.

Chapter eight: On the connection of existence with the substantiality of things *(shay'iyyah)*.

Chapter nine: On the various meanings of 'inhering existence' (*al-wujūd al-rābiṭī*).

The second 'way'–On the tripartite division of being (*al-mawādd al-thalāth*).

The 'way' consists of twenty-two chapters, of which the first twenty-one deal with the Necessary Being (*wājib al-wujūd*), contingent (or possible) being (*mumkin al-wujūd*) and impossible being (*mumtani' al-wujūd*) and the last with the unity of existence and quiddity objectively, that is, outside the mind. As for the third 'way', it consists of five chapters dealing with mental existence (*al-wujūd al-dhihnī*), which involves the question of knowledge.

The second stage, 'Supplements to the principles concerning existence and non-existence', is not divided into separate 'ways'. It consists directly of fourteen chapters dealing first with *wujūd*, then *'adam*, and finally *imkān* in the various meanings it possesses in Islamic philosophy.

Finally, the third stage deals with *ja'l*, the effect of the agent or cause upon the caused, which plays an important role in Mullā Ṣadrā's theosophy and complements his discussion of causality. The first three chapters of this stage deal with *ja'l* proper and the last two with the gradation of being.

With an awareness of the order in which Mullā Ṣadrā expounds his metaphysics we can now embark upon an analysis of the basic aspects of his doctrines by returning to the primary distinction between existence and quiddity.

The explanation of the distinction between existence and quiddity in the theosophy of Mullā Ṣadrā begins with an analysis of man's experience of the external world. In ordinary perception, man becomes aware of concrete things which exist in the objective world. But once man analyses this perception within his mind he realises that the concrete objects perceived can be analysed into two components: one which bestows reality upon the object, which is existence, and the other which determines the object to be what it is, which is its quiddity. Of course in the external world there is but one reality perceived, but within the mind the two components are clearly distinguishable. In fact, the mind can conceive clearly of a quiddity completely independently of whether it exists or not. Existence is an element added from the 'outside' to the quiddity. It is not part of the essential character of any quiddity in question save the Necessary Being, whose Being is none other than Its Quiddity. Existence and quiddity unite and through their union form objecs which at the same time exist and are also a particular thing.

Existence and quiddity can never be found separately in the external world. But in the analysis carried out by the mind the two elements are in fact totally different. They provide the key with which the mind can seek to understand the structure of reality.[13]

It is in the nature of the intellect *(al-'aql)* to unify (the word *'aql* itself in Arabic being related to the root meaning 'to bind' or 'unite') and to guide man from multiplicity to Unity. Sensory experience places man before the world of multiplicity, of objects that seem to be distinct and separate. It is the intellect which pierces through this veil of multiplicity and is able to distinguish between the permanent and the transient, substance and accidents, the Absolute and the relative, the Principle and its manifestation, the One and the many, and through this distinction to integrate multiplicity into Unity. The distinction between existence and quiddity is of such a nature. The intellect distinguishes between these two elements within each existent. This is the first stage in guiding man to the awareness of a reality which binds and also transcends individual objects, for the distinction between existence and quiddity leads in turn, in the theosophy of Mullā Ṣadrā, to the awareness of the inter- relatedness of existents and finally to the gradation, principiality and unity of being.

Before embarking upon his exposition of metaphysics, Mullā Ṣadrā seeks to show first of all that existence cannot be defined, that it is the most spontaneous, evident (*badīhī*) and basic of all realities and also concepts. He discusses this idea under the heading of *badāhat al-wujūd*, the 'spontaneity' or 'self-evidence of *wujūd*'. All things are known by it and so it cannot possess definition (*ta'rīf*) in terms of anything else. The logical definition which requires genus and specific difference is in fact impossible to apply in the case of *wujūd*, which is beyond every genus and specific difference, beyond internal division or composition upon which logical definition is based. The concept of existence is the most evident and primary concept in the mind, with the aid of which all other concepts are understood, and the reality of existence is the most immediate and primary experience of reality, an experience which is the foundation of all our knowledge of the external world. Hence how could one seek to define existence? Man's awareness of existence is immediate and intuitive. He is immersed in it and can gain an awareness of it only in an immediate, experiential manner which no mental analysis can hope to reach. Both the mental or subjective world and the external or objective one are encompassed by and plunged in the ocean of being and therefore cannot encompass or comprehend it. Existence in its purity can become neither an external object on the physical plane to be perceived nor a finite and bound concept in the mind to be logically defined, although it is the basis of every external object and the most evident and clear of all mental concepts.[14]

Having made the distinction between existence and quiddity and having pointed to the impossibility of defining existence in the usual sense of the word definition, Mullā Ṣadrā takes the first step towards an intellectual comprehension of the unity of things by proving that the term *wujūd* as used in the case of various things such as A, B and C refers to the same concept and reality and is not just based on verbal resemblance, as for example in the case of the word 'date' as used in the phrases 'the date of an event' and 'the date picked from a tree' which refers to completely different meanings but is verbally the same. According to Mullā Ṣadrā, when we say A exists and B exists, the word 'exist' is shared in meaning (*ishtirāk-i ma'nawī*) by A and B and not only in verbal form (*ishtirāk-i lafẓī* 'homonymy'), in contrast to what is claimed by so many of the *mutakallimūn* and earlier philosophers, who as far as the term *wujūd* is concerned do not pass beyond the level of homonymy. Mullā Ṣadrā offers many arguments in favour of the nature of 'existence' as possessing *ishtirāk-i ma'nawī*. This includes his reference to direct perception by the intellect according to which the difference between 'man exists' and 'an animal exists' is not the same as between, let us say, the sun and the moon. 'Exists' in the first sentence conveys a common and related meaning in the case of man and animal which is most direct and undeniable, so that even if in poetic rhyme the term *wujūd* is repeated, we naturally understand a similar meaning to be conveyed in each stanza, not as if several words with completely different meanings but only verbal resemblance were placed at the end of each verse. Moreover, the whole discussion of causality would become meaningless, were the term 'exists' in the phrase 'A exists' to have no relation in meaning to the term 'exists' in the phrase 'B exists', where A and B are causally related.[15]

Having established the reality of existence as reflected in human language, Mullā Ṣadrā turns to a distinction which is fundamental to his ontology and which characterises much of later Islamic philosophy in Persia, namely the distinction between the notion or concept (*mafhūm*) and the reality (*ḥaqīqah*) of existence.[16] When a general discussion concerning exisence takes place, people are not usually aware that they are in fact dealing with something on two very different planes of reality, reflecting the object-subject distinction of discursive knowledge itself. Transcendent theosophy insists on clarifying this primary distinction before embarking any further upon the difficult road of metaphysical exposition. It speaks of the notion of existence and the reality of existence. When a person says 'this house exists', he has an immediate notion of 'exists' at a pre-conceptual stage. The 'existence' of the house implied by the sentence is self-evident (*badīhī*). It is a notion that the mind knows directly and immediately. It is in fact the most evident of all notions, that which is known better and more directly, than anything else.[17] Its knowledge is so evident that everyone has an intuitive awareness of what it means before conceptualising it in his mind. All discursive and conceptualised knowledge concerning 'existence' follows later and is based upon that immediate 'understanding of existence' which is in fact implied by the term *mafhūm* itself in Arabic, meaning 'that which is understood'.

In contrast to this notion of existence in the mind, the reality of existence is the most difficult of all things to know in depth, for it requires a spiritual preparation which not all people possess, to say the least. Everyone with a sane mind has an intuitive grasp of the reality of existence, but only in its most outward mode. Everyone at the stage of immediate perception knows that when he perceives that a house exists, the existence of the house is not only a notion in his mind but also a reality independent of him.[18] If he is a contemplative, he becomes aware of this profound mystery of existence itself or of being in its virginal purity, which is like the Divine Breath that animates all things from within or like the Divine Ocean into which all things are plunged. He becomes conscious of Universal Existence which is itself the effusion of Pure Being and ultimately of the Divine Essence.[19] If he is not a contemplative he is nevertheless aware of the presence of the reality of existence, even if the remarkable mystery of existence becomes veiled before his dulled vision. Moreover, because being possesses various stages and grades, as we shall discuss soon, the higher realms remain inaccessible to the untrained mind and eye, and its root or *kunh* to which Sabziwārī refers in the poem already cited remains the most hidden of all things, for this root is none other than Pure Being Itself, which none can know except those who have lost their separative existence and become 'united' with it.

The reality of existence in its deepest aspect is, therefore, at the antipode of the notion of existence as far as man's approach through the usual channels of knowledge is concerned, the first being the most inaccessible and the second the most evident of all things. But this rapport is true only from the point of view of discursive knowledge and the modes of perception of 'fallen man'. For the spiritual man whose eye of the heart (*'ayn al-qalb* or *chishm-i dil*) has opened through spiritual discipline and Divine Succour, the most certain and evident of all things is precisely that root of the reality of existence which is the Source and Origin of all things and before which the self-evidence of all mental notions pales into insignificance. Mullā Ṣadrā is fully aware of this reversal of relationships in the case of spiritual vision and alludes to it in many parts of his work. But because his *ḥikmat al-muta'āliyah* has the function of guiding the perceptive mind to the doors of spiritual vision and the experience of the reality of existence, he begins with the distinction between the notion and the reality of existence and the self-evidence of the first in contrast to the hiddenness of the second. But his final goal is to lead man to the stage in which he can have that vision of the reality of existence which transforms the most hidden to the most manifest and the manifest to a pale shadow of that which first appeared as the most hidden and unknown.

One of the cardinal doctrines of Mullā Ṣadrā is the gradation of being (*tashkīk al-wujūd*) according to which being possesses various levels of reality which encompass ultimately not only the reality of existence but even its notion, which belongs in fact to a particular form of existence called mental existence (*wujūd-i dhihnī*). The doctrine of the gradation of being, stretching from Pure Being to *materia prima*, in the form expounded by Mullā Ṣadrā marks a major transformation in Islamic philosophy, although it is related to the universal doctrine of the 'great chain of being' found in various traditions both ancient and medieval[20] and more particularly to the concept of the gradation of light found in Suhrawardī.[21] Mullā Ṣadrā took this universal doctrine and made of it a cornerstone of his transcendent theosophy, interpreting it in the light of his particular version of the *philosophia perennis*.

Analogical gradation or analogicity (*tashkīk*) is interpreted in the school of Mullā Ṣadrā to mean that a single universal is predicable in different degrees and grades of its particulars.[22] The example often cited is that of light which is predicable of 'the light of the sun', 'the light of the lamp' and 'the light of the candle'. In each case one is dealing with light, but in each case in a different degree of intensity. If we ponder the concept of analogical gradation we will discover, however, that there is not one but two kinds of gradation: the first is one in which what causes the difference (*mā bihi'l-ikhtilāf*) in various degrees of something partaking of gradation is the same as that which these degrees or grades share in common (*mā bihi'l-ishtirāk*), for example, numbers or light. Both the number two and three are grades of the 'universal' number. Moreover, what they have in common is numerality and what separates them is also numerality. The same holds true of light. This type of gradation is called *tashkīk-i khāṣṣi* or particular gradation. The second is one in which what various grades share in common is not what separates them from each other, such as the existence of Abraham and Moses. What these two prophets share in common is existence but what separates them is their separation in time as well as other factors. This second type of analogical gradation is called *tashkīk-i 'āmmī* or general gradation.

When this analysis is applied to existence, it becomes clear that the notion of existence partakes of general gradation but the reality of existence partakes of particular gradation. When we think of the existence of A and existence of B in our mind, the notion of the existence of A and the notion of the existence of B share the notion of existence in common, but are separated by other factors. But the reality of existence is a single reality partaking of grades, so that which distinguishes the existence of A from the existence of B is the reality of existence and what unites them is also the reality of existence. This is the basis of the doctrine of the 'transcendent unity of being' (*waḥdat al-wujūd*) which crowns Mullā Ṣadrā's metaphysics and to which we shall turn shortly.

Of major importance for an understanding of Mullā Ṣadrā's metaphysics is his exposition of the relation between existence and quiddity. This problem, which was of major concern to the Latin Scholastics as well as to the Muslim Peripatetics, as already mentioned, goes back to al-Fārābī and Ibn Sīnā who wrote extensively about it.[23] Both men realised that when we say A exists, existence is from the linguistic and logical point of view an accident (*'araḍ*) added to the particular quiddity in question, and that it is unlike other predicates in that it does not tell anything additional about the subject. In the *Tahāfut al-tahāfut*[24] in his criticism of Ibn Sīnā, Ibn Rushd misconstrued the Avicennan position, interpreting existence to be an accident in the ordinary sense. Ibn Rushd in fact contributed in a major way to the misunderstanding of this aspect of Avicennan ontology in the West, and this fact in turn led indirectly to the inability of later Western philosophers to formulate an ontology of the depth and dimensions of a Mullā Ṣadrā.

Ibn Sīnā was in fact also misinterpreted on this account by certain Eastern philosophers and theologians such as Fakhr al-Dīn Rāzī, who interpreted Ibn Sīnā's reference to existence as a category to mean that it was a category like other categories such as quality and quantity. The true reviver of Ibn Sīnā's school in the East, Naṣīr al-Dīn Ṭūsī, was forced in fact to reject the Fakhrian interpretation of existence as an accident explicitly in his *Sharḥ al-ishārāt*.[25] Ibn Sīnā himself clarified his own words in his *Ta'līqāt*, which unfortunately never became known in the West but which were well-known to Mullā Ṣadrā, who in fact cites them when he wishes to discuss the question of the accidentality of existence.[26] By returning to this basic text of Ibn Sīnā whose very words he quotes[27] Mullā Ṣadrā is able to draw support from the master of Islamic Peripatetics for his own position concerning the reality of existence and in fact its principiality (*aṣālat*) as well, which follows from his doctrine concerning the reality of existence.

Mullā Ṣadrā's metaphysics is based on the thesis that although outwardly we see in the world objects that exist and for which existence is an accident added from the outside – as moreover human languages seem to imply – in reality there is but one Being with grades of existence issuing from It and stretching from Being Itself to the level of matter. With respect to this reality, it is not existence but the quiddities which are accidents. It *appears* that things exist; in reality, universal existence takes on the accidentality of things while remaining for ever within its primordial oneness and virginity. Using the language of Sufism, Mullā Ṣadrā calls this creative and expansive aspect of Universal Existence the 'Breath of the Compassionate' (*nafas al-raḥmān*) or the sacred effusion (*al-fayḍ al-muqaddas*) of which all things are but cosmic coagulations on various levels of cosmic reality. According to Mullā Ṣadrā, even Suhrawardī, the master of *ishrāq*, was not able to interpret this point in its true sense and so remained content with an 'essentialistic' metaphysics. It was for Mullā Ṣadrā to bring about this major transformation of metaphysics by realizing the true relation between existence and quiddity and becoming aware of the 'principiality of existence' (*aṣālat al-wujūd*), which is a major pillar of his metaphysics.

If one were to study *ḥikmat* with a traditional master in Persia to this day, one would be introduced early in one's studies to the distinction between the 'principiality of existence' (*aṣālat al-wujūd*) and the 'principiality of quiddity' (*aṣālat al-māhiyyah*).

Moreover, it is usually said that not only Mullā Ṣadrā but also Ibn Sīnā was a follower of *aṣālat al-wujūd* and that Suhrawardī and Mīr Dāmād belonged to the school of *aṣālat al-māhiyyah*. In fact, the whole of Islamic philosophy would be viewed from this perspective and divided accordingly. Among contemporary *ḥakīms* also the same classification is made, most being followers of *aṣālat al-wujūd*, and a few such as 'Allāmah Hā'irī Māzandarānī, the famous commentator of Ibn Sīnā who died fairly recently, belonging to the school of *aṣālat al-māhiyyah*.[28]

When we study the actual texts of earlier Islamic philosophy, however, we find that no such idea is ever expressed in them explicitly. A historical study will show that the very idea of the principiality of either existence or quiddity came to the fore in the writings of Mīr Dāmād and became a major problem of Islamic philosophy only from the Safavid period onwards. The Safavid and later Islamic philosophers read this distinction back into the history of Islamic philosophy because of its central importance, and re-interpreted Islamic philosophy accordingly. The major question underlying this way of looking at ontology is whether the reality of an existent comes from its existence or from its quiddity; in other words, wether 'existence' as used for various existents is merely a mental construct (*i'tibārī*) and the quiddity possesses reality, or existence possesses reality and the quiddity is nothing but the limitations of a particular mode of existence abstracted by the mind. Suhrawardī was a keen defender of the *i'tibārī* nature of 'existence' and the reality of the quiddities, although he spoke of light in terms similar to those Mullā Ṣadrā used for *wujūd*. Mīr Dāmād, likewise, believed that quiddity and not existence, possessed reality. Both masters therefore created an 'essentialistic metaphysics' and became known as *aṣālat-i māhiyyatī*, the Persian term for those who uphold the principiality of quiddity.

In his youth Mullā Ṣadrā also belonged to this school. In fact he did not become *aṣālat-i wujūdī*, or a defender of the principiality of existence, simply through reasoning or mental reflection. The change came through a divine inspiration and with the aid of Heaven. It seems that Mullā Ṣadrā underwent a spiritual experience which enabled him to have a new vision of reality and to carry out that profound transformation of Suhrawardian metaphysics from an essentialistic doctrine to an 'existentialistic' (*wujūdī*) one, a transformation which is a veritable turning point in the history of Islamic thought.[29] In his *Kitāb al-mashā'ir*, Mullā

Ṣadrā describes his 'conversion' in these terms:

> In earlier days I was a passionate defender of the thesis of the principiality of quiddity and the *i'tibārī* nature of existence, until God provided me with guidance and permitted me to witness His demonstration. All of a sudden my spiritual eyes were opened and I was able to see that the truth of the matter was contrary to what the philosophers in general had held. Praise be to God who by means of the light of illumination guided me out of the darkness of the baseless idea (of the principiality of quiddity) and established the thesis (of the principiality of existence) firmly within me, a thesis which will never change in this world or the next.
>
> As a result (of this experience), (I now believe that) the existences are realities, while the quiddities are the permanent archetypes (*al-a'yān al-thābitah*) which have never smelt the fragrance of existence.[30] The existences are nothing but rays of light, radiated by the true Light which is the absolutely self-subsistent Being, except that each existence is characterised by a number of essential properties and intelligible qualities. It is these latter aspects which are known as quiddities.[31]

In these words, Mullā Ṣadrā expresses clearly the inspired origin of his belief in the principiality of existence, but in nearly all his discussions of the 'general principles' of the Transcendent Theosophy (*al-umūr al-'āmmah*), in such works as the *Asfār*, *al-Shawāhid al-rubūbiyyah*, *al-Mashā'ir* and *al-Mabda' wa'l-ma'ād*, he offers numerous proofs for this view, rejecting all the arguments of Suhrawardī and others in favour of the principiality of quiddity.[32] These arguments relate to the problem of *ja'l*, or the effect of the agent or cause upon the caused, priority and posteriority in cause and effect, existence as the source of goodness, etc. As an example one can mention the argument of priority and posteriority within one quiddity which is repeated often by Ṣadr al-Dīn. If a quiddity called (A) such as a fire causes another quiddity called (B) which is also a fire, both (A) and (B) must be said to be the same quiddity, both being fire. If we accept the principiality of quiddity, then reality resides in the quiddity, and at the same time we would have to concede that the cause precedes the effect. Therefore, the self-same quiddity fire is prior as cause (A) and posterior as effect (B). There must as a result exist an analogical gradation in one and the same quiddity which is impossible as proven by all Islamic philosophers. Therefore, the reality of a thing must belong to existence, which partaking of gradation, can be both prior and posterior, both cause and effect, united in both instances to the same quiddity, which happens to be fire in this case.

The importance of the doctrine of the 'principiality of existence' in the Transcendent Theosophy can hardly be overemphasized. Based upon a new inspired vision of reality, this doctrine became in turn a major pillar of Mullā Ṣadrā's metaphysics, one which he sought to demonstrate logically and one which itself became the basis for the demonstration of so many other aspects of his teachings. This doctrine transformed the 'Aristotelian mould' of earlier Islamic philosophy, making the subject of metaphysics not the existent (*ens*) but the act of existence itself (*esse*), and provided a new vision of the pro-foundest order of reality in which everything is viewed as the 'presence' (*ḥuḍūr* or *shuhūd*) of the act of *wujūd* or the Divine Command (*al-amr*) itself. Moreover, it was through this doctrine that Mullā Ṣadrā was able to display the link that connects all the levels of reality together[33] and finally to bring to light the doctrine of the 'transcendent unity of being' (*waḥdat al-wujūd*) which crowns his whole metaphysics and in fact all of Islamic gnosis.[34]

The doctrine of the 'transcendent unity of being', contained implicitly in numerous Quranic verses and in the *Shahādah, Lā ilāha illa'Llāh*, itself, was not formulated in an explicit manner until the sixth/twelfth and seventh/thirteenth centuries when it appeared in the writings of Ibn 'Arabī and other masters of Islamic gnosis. Based upon the ineffable experience of annihilation (*al-fanā'*) and of unity (*al-tawḥīd*) at its highest level, the doctrine of *waḥdat al-wujūd* nevertheless gave rise to an even more refined intellectual formulation based on Ibn 'Arabī's didactic expositions. Various interpretations and ever more detailed analyses of its meaning appeared in the writings of Ṣadr al-Dīn al-Qūnawī, 'Abd al-Karīm al-Jīlī and many other sages of later centuries, including figures in Muslim India who developed particular formulations of this doctrine in the light of the challenges of Vedantic teachings.

Mullā Ṣadrā consummates his metaphysics based upon the principiality and gradation of being with the unity of being which lies at the heart of his doctrinal teachings. He elaborates upon various views concerning *waḥdat al-wujūd*, finally providing his own understanding of the doctrine which regards this Unity in the light of the gradation of being and of this gradation in the light of that Unity which not only unites all the levels of being but also transcends all that exists.[35]

The basis of Mullā Ṣadrā's metaphysics is thus the unity (*waḥdat*), principiality (*aṣālat*) and gradation (*tashkīk*) of being. The Universe issues from Pure Being through states which are all grades and levels of being separated from each other through the intensity or weakness of the light of being itself. Quiddities or what appear to be 'real things' are no more than abstractions made by the mind of the limits of various levels of being, limits which do not in any way prevent all these levels from being united together and in fact to Pure Being Itself. The vast expanses of universal manifestation are so many 'presences' or acts of existence which at once veil and reveal the One Being who alone is.

It should not be strange, therefore, to see Mullā Ṣadrā treating theology and theodicy (*ilāhiyyāt bi ma'na'l-khāṣṣ* or *rubūbiyyāt*) in nearly all of his works after having dealt with the general principles of metaphysics (*al-umūr al-'āmmah*). In reality 'the general principles' already contain the principles of theology and theodicy and are therefore treated before the sections which deal with God's Names and Attributes, His Unity and the like. Mullā Ṣadrā himself was a remarkable theologian as well as an outstanding *ḥakīm*, and separate works need to be devoted to his theological views. In fact, he was of the view that *kalām* is unfit to discuss the questions with which it concerned itself and that these questions are the proper domain of *ḥikmat* rather than *kalām*. But he was fully aware that the 'general principles' which form the heart of his metaphysical doctrines apply to all levels of reality, from Pure Being to the lowest level of existence, and to all realms of knowledge, from the knowledge of God and His Qualities and Attributes to the knowledge of the physical world. That is why he sought to provide with their help a key for an understanding of all branches of knowledge and to establish with their aid the basis of his transcendent theosophy. These principles apply to theology and theodicy as well as to cosmology, to ethics as well as to spiritual psychology and eschatology. All branches of Transcendent Theosophy, like those of any other traditional doctrine, are united to the trunk of a tree which is rooted in Being Itself and which is ultimately identifiable with the cosmic reverberations of Being, the tree to which the Noble Quran refers in the verse, 'a good tree, its roots set firm and its branches in heaven, giving its fruit at every season by the leave of its Lord' (Quran XIV: 24–5).

The metaphysical synthesis which has been briefly outlined here did not become philosophically dominant immediately, despite the fact that Mullā Ṣadrā had such illustrious students as Mullā Muḥsin Fayḍ Kāshānī and 'Abd al-Razzāq Lāhījī and that his teachings spread rapidly to India. An examination of the writings of Mullā Ṣadrā's own students reveals in fact that, probably because of political considerations, they dissimulated their attachment to their master's teachings and wrote mostly about either religious sciences such as Quranic commentary, *Ḥadīth* and *kalām* or Sufism and gnosis primarily in the form of poetry.[36] Lāhījī in fact expressly refuted such characteristic teachings of Mullā Ṣadrā as transsubstantial motion. Nevertheless, these figures must have continued to study and teach Mullā Ṣadrā's doctrines, some of which at least are reflected in such a work as Lāhījī's *Shawāriq*. Through them and their own students such as Qāḍī Sa'īd Qummī, the 'Transcendent Theosophy' of Mullā Ṣadrā must have been kept alive to the end of the Safavid period, despite the change in the religious climate which became more unfavourable towards such teachings during the years preceding the fall of the Safavids. It is said in fact that the golden chain of transmission of this school through the traditional master-disciple relationship became narrowed down to one or two figures, the most important being Mullā Muḥammad Ṣādiq Ardistānī who was banished from Isfahan just before the Afghan invasion.[37]

In any case, the school of Mullā Ṣadrā did not come to the fore in Persia until the early Qajar period when Mullā 'Alī Nūrī began to teach his works in Isfahan, the old capital which became once again the centre for the study of Mullā Ṣadrā, although the capital had now been moved to Tehran. Nūrī, who hailed originally from Māzandarān, was a most respected religious scholar, possessing sufficient stature to teach the works of Mullā Ṣadrā without facing any opposition from excessively exoteric religious scholars.[38] He taught the *Asfār* and other works of Ṣadr al-Dīn for over fifty years and by the time he had died in 1246 A H (lunar), he had not only written important works in the line of the school of Mullā Ṣadrā, but had also trained a whole new generation of philosophers who followed the Ṣadrian school. His commentaries upon Mullā Ṣadrā include glosses upon the *Asfār*, the *Mashā'ir* and the *Sharḥ uṣūl al-kāfī*.[39] Of those works, the elucidation of the difficult passages of the *Asfār* is particularly important.

The most important contribution of Nūrī is, however, the training of such outstanding masters of Islamic philosophy as Mullā Muḥammad Ismā'īl Iṣfahānī, Mullā 'Abdallāh Zunūzī, Mullā Muḥammad Ja'far Langarūdī, Mullā Ismā'īl Khājū'ī, and through them and other direct disciples the most famous of Qajar philosophers, that is, Ḥājjī Mullā Hādī Sabziwārī, Mullā 'Alī Mudarris Zunūzī and Āqā Muḥammad Riḍā Qumsha'ī. These figures made Ṣadrian metaphysics central to the teaching of Islamic philosophy in Qajar Persia, although it was not the only school, as is seen in the works of such figures as the Narāqīs and Mīrzā Abu'l-Ḥasan Jilwih. Even in the case of such 'non-Ṣadrian' philosophers and theologians of note, however, the influence of Mullā Ṣadrā can be felt.

Among the most important exponents of Ṣadrian metaphysics after Nūrī , namely Sabziwārī, Zunūzī , and Qumsha'ī, Sabziwārī was the only one not to migrate finally to Tehran which, following the death of Mullā 'Alī Nūrī, became the centre for the study of Islamic philosophy and remained so until the Pahlavi period and in fact throughout this century until recent times. Yet Sabziwārī is also the best known *ḥakīm* of the Qajar period and the only one about whom there are a few works in European languages.[40] The very popular philosophical poem of Sabziwārī, the *Sharḥ al-manẓūmah*, which summarises the teachings of Mullā Ṣadrā, soon became a favourite work on Islamic philosophy in traditional schools (*madrasahs*) throughout Persia, and remains to this day perhaps the most popular introduction to Islamic philosophy in that land. His commentary upon Mullā Ṣadrā's *al-Shawāhid al-rubūbiyyah* made this masterpiece of 'Transcendent Theosophy' much better known,[41] while Sabziwārī's Persian work, the *Asrār al-ḥikam*, helped to make Mullā Ṣadrā's teachings more accessible to those who could not master philosophical Arabic.[42] Through his radiant sanctity, intellectual rigour and poetic gifts Sabziwārī became one of the major intellectual and spiritual figures of Qajar Persia, a master whose teachings were simply the resuscitation of the doctrines of Mullā Ṣadrā.

Mullā 'Alī Zunūzī, a contemporary of Sabziwārī, who studied under his own father Mullā 'Abdallāh Zunūzī,[43] was the foremost exponent of Mullā Ṣadrā's teachings in Tehran during the later Qajar period and is considered as the most intellectually original figure of the Ṣadrian school during this period. Not only did he compose important glosses on major Islamic philosophical works such as the *Asfār* and the *Shifā'*, but he also wrote the *Badāyi' al-ḥikam* as an answer to questions posed to him by a Qajar prince, Badī' al-Mulk Mīrzā 'Imād al-Dawlah, who had learned about Kantian philosophy while travelling to Europe. This work represents the first confrontation between the school of Mullā Ṣadrā and modern European philosophy and deserves much greater attention than it has received until now. Āqā 'Alī Mudarris, as he was usually known, was also a Sufi initiate and occasionally composed poetry similar to his famous contemporary, Sabziwārī.[44]

As for Āqā Muḥammad Riḍā Qumsha'ī, he too migrated from Isfahan to Tehran, where he became known as the leading expositor of the gnosis of the school of Ibn 'Arabī while also teaching Mullā Ṣadrā and expounding his metaphysics. Many consider him in fact to be the greatest exponent of Ibn 'Arabī's school in Persia during the Qajar Period, and he is best known for his commentary upon the *Fuṣūṣ al-ḥikam* of Ibn 'Arabī as well as some of the works of Ibn 'Arabī's well-known commentator, Dā'ūd al-Qayṣarī.[45] At once an accomplished poet and a Sufi of the Dhahabiyyah order, Qumsha'ī represents the integral expression of Ibn 'Arabian gnosis in conjunction with Ṣadrian metaphysics and displays yet another facet of Islamic philosophy in Qajar Persia as it was influenced by Mullā Ṣadrā's metaphysics.

The famous philosophical figures of the late Qajar and early Pahlavi periods, such as Mīrzā Ṭāhir Tunakābunī and Mīrzā Mahdī Āshtiyānī, were students of these three great masters of Ṣadrian metaphysics and transmitted the teachings of Mullā Ṣadrā to the *ḥakīms* of the last two generations who have kept the flame of this school burning to the present day. Moreover, the most important intellectual and religious questions of the Qajar period such as the rise of new religious sects and schools, confrontation with Western thought and new educational experiments which were closely tied to the major social and political transformations of the late Qajar period and the Constitutional Revolution, were related to the revival of Mullā Ṣadrā's school during the Qajar period, when in fact it became more central and powerful than in the late Safavid period. No full understanding of the intellectual and religious life of Qajar Persia and in fact of post-Safavid Iran as a whole is possible without a better knowledge of the teachings and especially the metaphysics of Mullā Ṣadrā and their impact during the period of over three centuries which has passed since their first exposition by the sage from Shiraz. Besides their innate sapiential value, these teachings hold the key to the understanding of many facets of the intellectual life of Persians during that turbulent period when they were confronted for the first time with the full impact of Western civilisation and its challenge to the foundations of their own traditional culture and way of life.

Notes

1. The only serious studies on Islamic philosophy during the Qajar period in European languages are those of H. Corbin who, besides writing many essays, prepared in conjunction with S.J. Āshtiyānī the *Anthologie des philosophes iraniens*, Tehran-Paris, from 1972 onwards. Four of seven projected volumes of this anthology were completed before Corbin's death. Volume IV is of particular importance for the Qajar period although this volume lacks the analysis in French which Corbin had provided for the other volumes that set the background for the Qajar period. The French prolegomena have been assembled in his posthumous work *La philosophie iranienne islamique aux XVIIe et XVIIIe siècles*, Paris 1981.

   The work of T. Izutsu and M. Mohaghegh on Sabziwārī is also of great importance for an understanding of the philosophical thought of this period. See T. Izutsu, *The Concept and Reality of Existence*, Tokyo 1971; Mohaghegh and Izutsu, *The Metaphysics of Sabzavārī* Delmar (N.Y.) 1977; and their edition of *Sharḥ-i manẓūma*, Part 1, *Metaphysics*, Tehran 1969.

   See also S.H. Nasr, 'Sabziwārī', in M.M. Sharīf (ed.), *A History of Muslim Philosophy*, Wiesbaden 1966, II 1543–56.
2. For example in his *Sharḥ-i manẓūmah* he writes, while providing a proof for the gradation of existence according to Mullā Ṣadrā, "All that we hear from our contemporaries is nothing but sophistry based on a confusion between concepts and the objects to which they apply." Mohaghegh and Izutsu, *The Metaphysics of Sabzavārī*, 41–2.
3. On Mullā Ṣadrā see Nasr, *The Islamic Intellectual Tradition in Persia*, London, Curzon Press, 1996; Corbin, *En Islam iranien*, IV, 1972, 54–122; Corbin, *La Philosophie iranienne islamique*, 49–82; and J. W. Morris, trans., *The Wisdom of the Throne – An Introduction to the Philosophy of Mullā Ṣadrā*, Princeton 1981.
4. We must draw attention to the importance of terms used in this connection, considering the vast confusion that has arisen in European Languages since the end of the Middle Ages as a result of different ways in which 'being' and 'existence' have been used. In this exposition whenever we used 'Being' capitalised we mean the Absolute and Pure Being transcending the created order or particular existents. When we use 'Existence' capitalised we refer to that universal 'emanation' from Pure Being which forms the indifferentiated primordial substance of cosmic reality. Finally when we use 'existence' with a small 'e' we refer to particular things or to the principle of existence *vis-à-vis* quiddity, as for example the existence of a table or chair or the existence of an object in contrast to its quiddity. However, since Mullā Ṣadrā's whole metaphysics is based upon the unity and gradation of *wujūd* we shall also use 'being' in the lower case to refer to this graded aspect of reality which stretches from Being to individual existents. We hope to evoke through the use of this language the rapport of particular existents to Being Itself. In this latter

sense, being is closely related in meaning to existence in that it implies separation from Primordial Being; but it also implies union with the source and reflects the metaphysical principle that although the grades of being or existents are separated from Being Itself, they are also united with the Source. It must be remembered that existence (*ex-sistere*) means, as the Scholastics knew so well, subsistence by or through something else, namely through being (*ex alio sistere*). Our separation of the meaning of existence and Being in the sense that the first is based upon the second which is its Principle has nothing to do with the modern existentialist separation of the two terms. See Corbin's introduction to Mullā Ṣadrā, *Le Livre des pénétrations métaphysiques*, 77.

5. Corbin goes so far as to call Mullā Ṣadrā's transformation of earlier Islamic philosophy a 'revolution'. He writes 'Mullā Ṣadrā opère une révolution qui détrône la véritable métaphysique de l'essence, dont le règne durait depuis des siècles, depuis Fārābī, Avicenne et Sohrawardī.' *Le Livre des pénétrations métaphysiques*, 62.

6. Masters of the school of Mullā Ṣadrā always mention the principle that in *ḥikmat-i ilāhī* the active participle, the verb or infinitive and the passive participle of root forms are ultimately the same, for example, lover (*'āshiq*), love (*'ishq*), and the beloved (*ma'shūq*); he in whom intellection takes place (*'āqil*) the intellect (*'aql*) and the intelligible (*ma'qūl*); and He who gives existence (*wājid*), existence (*wujūd*) and the existent (*mawjūd*). But this is a later synthesising and unifying perspective characteristic of the school of Mullā Ṣadrā which cannot in any way obliterate the difference in perspective between the metaphysics of Ibn Sīnā, at least the Peripatetic Ibn Sīnā, and that of Mullā Ṣadrā.

7. See Izutsu, *The Concept and Reality of Existence*, Tokyo 1971, 68ff. This study contains a profound analysis of the ontology of Mullā Ṣadrā as seen in the writings of his great commentator Sabziwārī. We are fully in accord with the theses of this study, save for certain comparisons made by the author between the school of Mullā Ṣadrā and Western existentialism.

8. One must be very careful in making any comparisons between the ontology of Mullā Ṣadrā and modern existentialism despite some superficial resemblance concerning certain points. The metaphysics of Mullā Ṣadrā is based on the inner vision of Universal Existence before all of its cosmic coagulations, a vision that is made possible only through tradition and the spiritual means contained within it. Western existentialism cannot but be a parody and caricature of traditional metaphysics since its exponents such as Sartre or even Heidegger are totally cut off from those spiritual means which alone make that vision possible. The experience described by J-P. Sartre in *La nausée*, Paris 1938, 161ff., cannot but be of the reflection of the *materia prima* at the lower boundary of cosmic manifestation and at the very antipode of Universal Existence. It is, therefore, an error of a most dangerous kind to confuse the two. On the basic differences between the school of Mullā Ṣadrā and modern existentialism see Corbin, *Le Livre des pénétrations métaphysiques*, ch.IV, 62ff.

9. See F. Schuon, 'Ātmā-Māyā', *Studies in Comparative Religion*, Summer 1973, 130ff.

10. Mullā Ṣadrā, like earlier Islamic philosophers, distinguishes between *māhiyyah* 'in its most particular sense' (*bi'l-ma'na'l-akhaṣṣ*), which is in answer to the question 'what is it?' or *mā huwa* in Arabic, hence the word *māhiyyah* itself, and the meaning of *māhiyyah* 'in its most general sense' (*bi'l-ma'na 'l-a'amm*), which is in answer to 'what is the reality (*ḥaqīqah*) by which a thing is what it is?' (*mā bihi huwa huwa* in Arabic). See Mullā Ṣadrā, *Asfār*, first *Safar*, vol. II, 2ff. See also Izutsu, *op. cit.*, 101. Izutsu translates *māhiyyah* in its first sense as 'quiddity' and in its second sense as 'essence'.

11. For an excellent account of this subject in Western philosophy see E. Gilson, *L'Être et l'essence*, Paris 1948. Unfortunately, a similar treatment cannot be

found for Islamic philosophy. For Ibn Sīnā's views on the subject see A.M. Goichon, *La Distinction de l'essence et de l'existence d'après Ibn Sīna (Avicenna)*, Paris 1937.

12. For example in the *Mashā'ir*, which is devoted to ontology, the first four chapters (*mash'ars*) of Book One (*al-minhāj al-awwal*) are devoted to *wujūd* and only the fifth *mash'ar* to the relation between *wujūd* and *māhiyyah*. In the *Asfār*, however, the first *faṣl* of the second *maqālah* of the first *safar* is devoted to the distinction between existence and quiddity, and then after extensive discussion of existence and its *aḥkām*, in the fifth *maqālah*, he turns to the detailed analysis of quiddity and questions pertaining to it.
13. The discussion of *wujūd* and *māhiyyah* is so vast that no elementary discussion such as this can do justice to it. In fact, in as much as the understanding of the theosophy of Mullā Ṣadrā presumes a knowledge of Avicennan philosophy, concerning the question of *wujūd* and *māhiyyah* also we expect the reader to have some acquaintance with the discussions of the earlier Islamic philosophers on the subject in order to grasp the discussion at hand.
14. On the impossibility of defining *wujūd* see *Asfār*, first *safar*, vol.I, 83ff.; *al-Mashā'ir*, 6ff. In *al-Shawāhid al-rubūbiyyah* he says,

»الوجود لايمكن تصوّره بالحدّ ولابالرسم ولا بصورة مساوية له اذ تصوّر الشيء العينيّ عبارة عن حصول معناه وانتقاله من حدّالعين الى حدّ الذهن. فهذا يجرى فى غيرالوجود. و امّا فى‌الوجود فلايمكن ذلک الاّ بصريح المشاهدة وعين العيان دون اشارةالحدّ والبرهان وتفهيم العبارة والبيان.«

15. On the discussion of *ishtirāk-i ma'nawī* and reasons brought forward in its support, see *Asfār* first *safar*, vol.I, 35–6.
16. This theme runs throughout the first *safar* of the *Asfār* and is especially emphasised in Sabziwārī's summary of Mullā Ṣadrā's doctrines in *sharḥ al-manẓūmah*. For a detailed analysis of this distinction in reference to both Mullā Ṣadrā and Sabziwārī see Izutsu, *op. cit.*, 68ff.
17. That is why Sabziwārī, summarising the teachings of Mullā Ṣadrā, says in his *Sharḥ al-manẓūmah* edited by Izutsu and Mohaghegh, Tehran 1969, 4,

مفهومه من أعرف الاشياء   و كنهه فى غاية الخفاء

18. Of course, Mullā Ṣadrā was aware of the argument of the sollipsist and the subjectivist, which he refutes through various arguments. But in making this distinction between the notion and reality of existence he is appealing precisely to our immediate perception of reality and not to whatever conceptual schemes certain philosophical minds of other tendencies may have imposed upon that immediate perception.
19. On 'sacred effusion' (*fayḍ-i muqaddas*) and 'most sacred effusion' (*fayḍ-i aqdas*) used by Ṣūfīs of the school of Ibn 'Arabī as well as Mullā Ṣadrā see Ibn 'Arabī, *La Sagesse des prophètes*, trans. by T. Burckhardt, Paris 1955, 23–4.
20. For an exposition of this doctrine in ancient philosophy and the West see A. Lovejoy, *The Great Chain of Being*, Cambridge (U S A) 1936; see also S.H. Nasr, *Knowledge and the Sacred*, Edinburgh 1981, ch.4.
21. Suhrawardī in his ontology bestowed all reality upon the *māhiyyāt* and believed existence to be a mere accident, but as already mentioned by many scholars, spoke of light (*al-nūr*) in terms that make it synonymous with being. As far as light is concerned, he spoke explicitly of its gradation and is in fact the first Islamic philosopher to have given a rational demonstration of the possibility of *tashkīk*, answering the criticisms Ibn Sīnā and other Peripatetics had given against it. Mūlla Ṣadrā took Suhrawardī's concept of *tashkīk* as applied to light and applied it to *wujūd*. See Suhrawardī, *Ḥikmat al-ishrāq*, ed. by Corbin, Tehran–Paris 1952, 119–20. That is why in his *Sharḥ al-manẓūmah* Sabziwārī attributes *tashkīk* to the ancient Persian sages' (the *fahlawiyyūn*) saying,

الفهلويّون الوجود عندهم حقيقة ذات تشكّك تعمّ

Izutsu and Mohaghegh edition, 5.

22. On *tashkīk*, see *Asfār*, first *safar*, vol.I, 423 ff.; also Izutsu, *The Concept and Reality of Existence*, 138ff. In his fine discussion on *tashkīk*, M. Ilāhī Qumsha'ī says, 'The meaning of *tashkīk* is realised whenever a single "truth" (*ḥaqīqah*) is predicable of its particulars in different degrees',

معنی تشکیک آنگاه محقق شود که حقیقت واحدی بر افراد کثیر بتفاوت صدق کند

M. Ilāhī Qumshā'ī, *Ḥikmat-i ilāhī khāṣṣ wa 'āmm*, Tehran 1335 (A. H. solar), 9.

23. Al-Fārābī discusses it in his *Risālah li'l-mu'allim al-thānī fī jawāb masā'il su'ila 'anhu*, and Ibn Sīnā in several of his works including *al-Ishārāt wa'l-tanbīhāt*. See Izutsu, *op. cit.*, chapters 3–6 where this whole question is thoroughly analyzed.
24. See *Tahāfut al-tahāfut*, ed. by S.van Den Bergh, London 1954, 1,237; also Izutsu, *op. cit.*, 81.
25. The appropriate passage has been translated into English by Izutsu in his *The Concept and Reality of Existence*, 121–2.
26. The *Ta'līqāt*, which is a major work of Ibn Sīnā and necessary for an understanding of many facets of his thought, has been neglected in contemporary research on him and only recently appeared in its first printing, ed. by A. Badawī, Cairo 1973.
27. See Mullā Ṣadrā, *Kitāb al-mashā'ir*, ed. by Corbin, 34, 83 and 84 where he quotes the words of Ibn Sīnā to show that the particular 'accident' we call existence is such that 'its existence in a substratum is the very existence of that substratum' (وجوده في موضوعه نفس وجود موضوعه) unlike other accidents which need a substratum that already possesses existence in order to become existent. It is of interest to note that immediately following the quotation from the *Ta'līqāt*, Mullā Ṣadrā describes his conversion to the school of the 'principiality of existence'.
28. All the *ḥakīms* of Persia have been followers of either one school or the other except Shaykh Aḥmad Ahsā'ī, the founder of the Shaykhī School, who thought one could uphold the principiality of both existence and quiddity at the same time. The impossibility of such a view has been demonstrated by followers of both schools.
29. See note 5 above for Corbin's description of this transformation as a revolution in Islamic philosophy.
30. This is in reference to the famous words of Ibn 'Arabī ,

«الاعيان الثابتة ما شمّت رائحة الوجود.»

see *La Sagesse des prophètes*, 67.

31. *Mashā'ir*, ed. by Corbin, p.35 of the Arabic text. Corbin's translation of this passage into French appears on p.152 of the French part of the book . There is an English translation of this passage in Izutsu, *The Concept and Reality of Existence*, 104, which we have followed closely with certain changes.

   It is of great interest to note, as Corbin has already pointed out in the above source, that Suhrawardī uses nearly the same terms in his *Ḥikmat al-ishrāq*, 156–7, to show how he was awakened from the limited confines of Peripatetic philosophy to become aware of the luminous world to which *ishrāqī* theosophy is devoted.
32. For arguments in defence of *aṣālat al-wujūd* see especially the *Asfār*, first *safar*, 38ff. These arguments have been summarised by Mullā Ṣadrā in the *Mashā'ir*, 37ff. The arguments given by Sabziwārī in his *Sharḥ al-manẓūmah*, 4 and 43–6, are also taken from Mullā Ṣadrā's demonstrations. The arguments of Mullā Ṣadrā have been likewise analysed and summarised by S.J. Āshtiyānī in

his *Hasti az naẓar-i falsafah wa 'irfān*, Mashhad 1379 (A. H. lunar), 205ff.

33. In a sense the two schools of the principiality of existence and principiality of quiddity in later Islamic philosophy correspond to the views based on the continuity and discontinuity of cosmic reality, or the substance and the essence. The first school emphasizes more the gradation and stages of being of the one Divine Substance from whose matrix all multiplicity flows forth while preserving its primordial unity (although in terms of Islamic philosophy *wujūd* is considered to be above the category of *jawhar* or substance as usually understood). The second school emphasizes the discontinuity of things, their separate essences which reflect the divine possibilities on the cosmic plane.
34. On the centrality of the doctrine of *waḥdat al-wujūd* in Islamic gnosis see Nasr, *Science and Civilisation in Islam*, Cambridge (U S A) 1968, New York 1970, ch. 13.
35. We have dealt extensively with Mullā Ṣadrā's doctrine of the 'transcendent unity of being' in Nasr, *Islamic Life and Thought*, London 1981, ch. 16, 'Mullā Ṣadrā and the doctrine of the unity of being.'
36. See the Persian introductions of Āshtiyānī to vols I and II of the *Anthologie des philosophes iraniens*; and Corbin, *La Philosophie iranienne islamique*, 96ff. and 179ff.
37. On Ardistānī and his role in the transmission of the teachings of Mullā Ṣadrā to the Zand and Qajar periods, see Āshtiyānī, *Anthologie....* vol. IV, 2ff.
38. On Nūrī, see M. Ṣadūqī Suhā, *A Bio-Bibliography of Post-Ṣadr-ul-Muta'allihīn Mystics and Philosophers*, Tehran 1980, 33–40; and Ashtiyānī, *Anthologie...*, vol. IV, 139ff.
39. On these works of Mullā Ṣadrā, see chap. 2 of this work.
40. See the works of Izutsu, Mohaghegh and Nasr already cited as well as the English preface of Nasr and the Persian introduction of S.J. Āshtiyānī to his edition of Sabziwārī, *Rasā'il*, Mashhad 1970; and the introduction of Izutsu to the Mohaghegh and Falāṭūrī edition of M.M. Āshtiyānī's *Commentary on Sabzawārī's Sharḥ-i manẓūmah*, Tehran 1973.
41. See the English preface of Nasr to S.J. Āshtiyānī's edition of *al-Shawāhid ul-rubūbiyyah* with the complete glosses of Sabziwārī, Mashhad 1967.
42. A notable feature of Islamic philosophy during the Qajar period is the revival of Persian as a vehicle for philosophical writings going back in a sense to the pre-Safavid period from the time of Nāṣir-i Khusraw and Suhrawardī onwards, when Persian prose witnessed its golden age and when most of the philosophical masterpieces of Persian prose were produced. Many Persian philosophical texts of the Qajar period remain to be edited and studied including some of the translations of the works of Mullā Ṣadrā from Arabic into Persian.
43. Mullā 'Abdallāh was himself a notable Ṣadrian philosopher especially interested in questions of eschatology. See the introduction of Nasr to Āshtiyānī's edition of *Lama'āt-i ilāhiyyah*, Tehran 1976.
44. On Mullā 'Alī, see Ṣadūqī, Suhā *op. cit.*, 155ff.
45. See the introduction of S.J. Āshtiyānī to his edition of *Rasā'il-i Qayṣarī*, Tehran 1357 (A.H. solar), which includes Āqā Muḥammad Riḍā's important treatise on *walāyah*.

Chapter 7

The Quranic Commentaries of Mullā Ṣadrā

As yet little attention has been paid in the West to the Quranic commentaries of Mullā Ṣadrā which are of great significance from the point of view of both the history of Quranic commentary and Islamic philosophy[1] and even in Persia interest in them is recent. Without doubt these commentaries are the most important by an Islamic philosopher or theosopher (*ḥakīm*) and also the most voluminous by a representative of the Islamic philosophical tradition until the present century when a follower of the school of Mullā Ṣadrā, 'Allāmah Sayyid Muḥammad Ḥusayn Ṭabāṭabā'ī (d. 1983), wrote his monumental *Tafsīr al-mīzān.*

Even in Persia, the home of Mullā Ṣadrā and his school, until the past fifteen years most attention to his works were concentrated upon his properly speaking philosophical works such as the *Asfār* and *al-Shawāhid al-rubūbiyyah* and the Quranic commentaries did not receive as much attention as the philosophical texts or even Mullā Ṣadrā's commentary upon the *Uṣūl al-kāfī* of Kulaynī. Since 1980, however, thanks most of all to the indefatigable efforts of Muḥammad Khwājawī, the different commentaries, all in Arabic, have been published in new editions usually with Persian translations both as separate volumes and together in a collected work which the editor has entitled *Tafsīr al-qur'ān al-karīm.*[2]

In the same way that Mullā Ṣadrā's "Transcendent Theosophy" marks the synthesis of the various schools of gnosis, theosophy, philosophy and theology within a Shi'ite intellectual climate, his Quranic commentaries mark the meeting point of four different traditions of Quranic commentary before him, the Sufi, the Shi'ite, the theological and the philosophical.[3] Both Sufi and Shi'ite commentaries trace their origin to the comment–

aries of Imams Muḥammad al-Bāqir and Ja'far al-Ṣādiq, which in turn go back to 'Alī about whom Ibn 'Abbās was to say, "What I took from the interpretation of the Quran is from 'Alī ibn Abī Ṭālib."[4] The 3rd/9th century Egyptian Sufi Dhu'l-Nūn al-Miṣrī made an edition of Imam Ja'far's *tafsīr* and was the spiritual predecessor of Sahl al-Tustarī, the author of the oldest extant continuous Sufi commentary upon the Quran.[5] The same *tafsīr* was given a new recension by Ibn 'Aṭā', a recension that was later incorporated by Sulamī in the 4th/10th century in his *Ḥaqā'iq al-tafsīr*, the second oldest Sufi Quranic commentary after Tustarī.

From this early tradition there flowed the major Sufi commentaries of later centuries such as the *Laṭā'if al-ishārāt* of Imam Abu'l-Qāsim al-Qushayrī and the commentary of Khwājah 'Abdallāh Anṣārī in the 5th/11th century. The latter was completed and much expanded in the monumental Sufi commentary of Anṣārī's student, Rashīd al-Dīn Maybudī, which is one of the masterpieces of the Persian language. The next two centuries were witness to the continous flowering of this tradition with the appearance of the two colossal figures of Abū Ḥāmid Muḥammad al-Ghazzālī and Rūzbihān Baqlī Shīrāzī, whose *'Arā'is al-bayān* brings this early chapter of Sufi Quranic commentary to its culmination and close.

A new chapter in Sufi Quranic commentaries was inaugurated a generation after Baqlī by Muḥyī al-Dīn ibn 'Arabī who left a most profound mark upon all later esoteric commentaries and particularly on those of Mullā Ṣadrā. The *Futūḥāt al-makkiyyah* of Ibn 'Arabī is in so many ways a Quranic commentary and brings out and over again some of the most profound meanings of the verses of the Sacred Book.[6] Ibn 'Arabī is also the author of a monumental commentary that is as yet unpublished while the well-known commentary, *Ta'wīl al-qur'ān,* attributed to him, belongs to the 8th/14th century follower of his school, 'Abd al-Razzāq Kāshānī. In any case this long Sufi tradition of *Tafsīr* and *ta'wīl* was well-known to Mullā Ṣadrā and constitutes one of the four traditions of Quranic commentary which became wed together in his own works on the subject.

The second tradition, namely the Shi'ite, also begins with the work of Imam Ja'far al-Ṣādiq and includes not only more formal and "external" commentaries such as *al-Tibyān fī tafsīr al-qur'ān* of Abū Ja'far Muḥammad al-Ṭūsī and *Majma' al-bayān fī tafsīr al-qur'ān* of Abū 'Alī al-Faḍl al-Ṭabarsī, but also works of Shi'ite gnostics such as the 8th/14th century figure Ḥaydar Āmulī and his successor in the 9th/15th century Ṣā'in al-Dīn ibn Turkah Iṣfahānī. Again Mullā Ṣadrā may be said to stand directly within this tradition with which he was very familiar, being himself a Shi'ite gnostic and philosopher of the highest order. This tradition is also to be seen in the works of some of Mullā Ṣadrā's contemporaries and students such as Sayyid Aḥmad 'Alawī and Mullā Muḥsin Fayḍ Kāshānī.

As far as theological commentaries, by which we mean commentaries associated with the schools of *kalām*, are concerned, it is necessary to state that Mullā Ṣadrā was in general opposed to *kalām* as such and believed that the *mutakallimūn* had no right to deal with the subjects with which they were for the most part engaged, and that these subjects, having to do with God, His Names and Attributes, the human soul, etc., should be treated by the "theosophers" (*ḥukamā-yi ilāhī*) who had access to divine inspiration as well as reason and the external form of the revelation. Nevertheless, Mullā Ṣadrā was closely familiar with *kalām* especially the works of Ghazzālī and Fakhr al-Dīn Rāzī among the Ash'arites and the *Tajrīd* of Naṣīr al-Dīn Ṭusī in Shi'ite *kalām*. As far as Quranic commentaries from the perspective of *kalām* are concerned, however, it is especially the *Tafsīr al-kabīr* of Fakhr al-Dīn Rāzī that must be mentioned. Like nearly all later Quranic commentators, Sunni and Shi'ite alike, Mullā Ṣadrā knew of this immense commentary and most likely had studied ot least parts of it.[7] One can see also traces of Ghazzālī's methodology of commentary upon the Quran in Mullā Ṣadrā, this influence being predominantly from the Sufism of Ghazzālī but also to some extent from the aspect of the thought of Ghazzālī as an Ash'arite.

Finally, a word must be said about philosophical commentaries upon the Quran by which we mean commentaries written by those technically called *faylasūf* or *ḥakīm*. Already in al-Fārābī there is some concern with Quranic commentary especially if we accept the *Fuṣūṣ al-ḥikmah* as being by him. But the founder of philosophical commentary in the Islamic intellectual tradition is Ibn Sīnā who not only wrote separate commentaries upon verses of the Quran, but also provided a famous commentary upon the "Light Verse" in his *al-Ishārāt wa'l-tanbīhāt* which influenced even Ghazzālī's *Mishkāt al-anwār* despite the latter's opposition to Avicennan philosophy. Strangely enough, however, this corpus has not been taken as seriously as it should in most of the studies on Ibn Sīnā in the West, and even in most of the contemporary Islamic scholarship on the subject.[8]

After Ibn Sīnā, it was especially Suhrawardī who turned to the Quran in his exposition of *ishrāqī* doctrine. In contrast to Ibn Sīnā, however, Suhrawardī did not write separate Quranic commentaries, but his works are replete with Quranic quotations upon which he comments amidst his exposition of various philosophical and theosophical theses in contrast to Ibn Sīnā who did not quote the Quran directly in such major works as the *Shifā'* and *Najāt*.

Mullā Ṣadrā's commentaries may be said to be a synthesis of all these four schools of Quranic commentary with which he had various degree of familiarity and the situation of his commentaries in the context of the history of Quranic commentary cannot be understood except in the context of these schools. Of course Mullā Ṣadrā was also acquainted with the standard commentaries common among Muslim scholars such as those of Bayḍāwī, Ṭabarī, Zamakhsharī and Abu'l-Futūḥ al-Rāzī. But one should not think for one moment that Mullā Ṣadrā's commentaries are simply an eclectic gathering of elements from these commonly known commentaries and the four particular traditions of Quranic commentary mentioned above, namely, the Sufi, the Shi'ite, the theological and the philosophical, any more than the *ḥikmat al-muta'āliyah* is simply the sum of the teachings of the schools which preceded it. In many of his Quranic commentaries Mullā Ṣadrā states that this or that meaning was unveiled to him by inspiration from the Divine Throne and that no one will be able to understand the inner meaning of the Quran without that unveiling *(kashf)* which enables the "eye of the heart" to gaze directly upon the realities of the spiritual world and even beyond them to the Divine Reality from which the Quran has descended.

* * *

The Quranic commentaries of Mullā Ṣadrā are as follows[9]:

1. Commentary upon chapter *LVII*, *al-Ḥadīd* (Iron), with one introduction, twenty nine parts[10] and a conclusion.
2. Commentary upon the "Throne Verse," *(āyat al-kursī)*, *(II; 255)*, one of his longest and most important commentaries consisting of an introduction and twenty chapters.
3. Commentary upon the "Light Verse," *(āyat al-nūr)*, *(XXIV; 35)*. Consisting of an introduction, a prolegomena, five chapters

and a conclusion, this work is in a sense the synthesis and peak of the long tradition of commentaries upon this verse and is one of the major works of Islamic metaphysics.

4. Commentary upon chapter *XXXII, al-Sajdah* (The Prostration), consisting of an introduction, a prolegomena, nine parts and a conclusion.

5. Commentary upon chapter *I, al-Ḥamd* or *al-Fātiḥah* (The Opening), consisting of five parts in which the various meanings of *bismi'Llāh* with which the chapters of the Quran begin are discussed.

6. Commentary upon chapter *II, al-Baqarah* (The Cow) which was completed only up to verse sixty six and in which he refutes many of the these of the Ash'arites and Mu'tazilites.

7. Commentary upon chapter *XXXVI Ya-Sīn* (Y-S) consisting of eight principles to prove bodily resurrection followed by sixteen chapters.

8. Commentary upon chapter *LXII, al-Jum'ah* (The Congregation) consisting of an introduction, twelve parts and several "inspirations from the Divine Throne" *(al-ḥikmat al-'arshiyyah)*, gnostic affirmation and a conclusion.

9. Commentary upon chapter *LV, al-Wāqi'ah* (The Event), consisnting of an introduction followed by the text, the introduction containing autobiographical material about his journey from the outward to the inward.

10. Commentary upon chapter *LXXXVI, al-Ṭāriq* (The Morning Star), consisting of an introduction and the text in which he states there are great secrets hidden in this chapter unveiled to him by God.

11. Commentary upon chapter *LXXXVII, al-A'alā* (The Most High), with an introduction and seven chapters.

12. Commentary upon chapter *XCIX, al-Zilzāl* (The Earthquake), with an introduction and the text.

In addition to these commentaries there are three works of Mullā Ṣadrā which are directly related to the subject at hand. The first and by far the most important is *Mafātīḥ al-ghayb* which is one of Mullā Ṣadrā's most important works ranking with the *Asfār, al-Shawāhid al-rubūbiyyah* and *Sharḥ uṣūl al-kāfī*. In it he speaks of his method in the interpretation of the Quran (especially in the first two chapters, that is, *al-miftāḥ al-awwal* and *al-miftāḥ al-thānī*). Secondly there is the *Mutashābihāt al-qur'ān* which summarizes the discussion of the *Mafātiḥ al-ghayb* as far as the "ambiguous" verses of the Quran are concerned. Finally there is *Asrār al-āyāt* which contains a section on the esoteric meaning of the abbreviated letters at the beginning of certain chapters of the Quran.

It must not be thought, however, that these fifteen works taken together contain all of Mullā Ṣadrā's Quranic commentaries. To include all of his commentaries one must also include the many verses quoted and commented upon in such philosophical works as the *Asfār, al-Shawāhid al-rubūbiyyah al-Mashā'ir, al-Mabda' wa'l-ma'ād, al-Ḥikmat al-'arshiyyah,* etc. As we have had occasion to remark before[11], although Mullā Ṣadrā's works can be categorized into those dealing with the intellectual sciences (*al-'ulūm al-aqliyyah*) and those dealing with the transmitted sciences (*al-'ulūm al-naqliyyah*), this categorization is not based on matual exclusion. The predominantly *'aqlī* works still possess *naqlī* elements and vice-versa. Therefore, in a sense the whole corpus of Mullā Ṣadrā is related to Quranic commentary while all of his Quranic commentaries are replete with philosophical and theosophical discussions. The works cited above, however, constitute his Quranic commentaries in a more exclusive sense and should be studied precisely as Quranic commentary. In fact together they constitute one of the major intellectual and gnostic commentaries upon the Quran in Islamic history.

* * *

The method of Mullā Ṣadrā in his Quranic commentaries is based on the avoidance of both pitfalls of remaining bound only by the outer meaning of the Sacred Text and of neglecting or negating the outward and formal meaning altogether. While at the beginning of his commentary, upon *Sūrat al-sajdah*, he expresses his opposition to those satisfied only with the external meaning of the Text, in his commentary upon *Ayat al-nūr* he criticizes those who, in the name of carrying out *ta'wīl*[12], pay no attention to the external meaning of Quranic terms as those words are understood in ordinary language. He even goes so far as to claim that such interpreters and commentators *(mu'awwil)* are more dangerous than those who limit the Quran simply to its outward meaning.[13]

According to Mullā Ṣadrā, authentic Quranic commentary is possible only for those whom the Quran calls "firm in knowledge" *(al-rāsikhūn fi'l-'ilm).* Even among this exalted group of people of knowledge, there is a hierarchy and levels of understanding, some being able to reach more inner meanings of the text than others. But even the highest among those "firm in knowledge" cannot gain access to the whole meaning of the Quran. The highest and profoundest meaning of the Sacred Text is know to God alone. On all levels, moreover, what those "firm in knowledge" utter about the meaning of the Text is not opposed to the outward meaning (*al-ẓāhir*) but complements it. To reach the inner meaning is not to oppose the outward sense.

Authentic Quranic commentaries must rely on two basic sources: clear transmission of the text of the Quran and vision of the truth which is so evident as not to be open to doubt or refutation. This latter source he identifies with unveiling (*mukāshafah*) and knowledge received by the heart (*al-wāridāt al-qalbiyyah*), terms which are used often by Mullā Ṣadrā to refer to knowledge received through intellection and illumination. To gain full access to this latter source, the commentator must undergo ascetic practices and self-purification. Otherwise he is simply fooling himself. Despite being an outstanding speculative philosopher, Mullā Ṣadrā insists that when it comes to the Quran, ordinary use of reason as understood by rationalistic philosophers is not sufficient. The heart must be purified and illuminated before the inner meaning of the Quran can be understood and transmitted. In his commentary upon the *āyat al-kursī* he goes so far as to say that he is addressing only the elite among the people of God (*ahl Allāh*), the lovers of God and those who believe in what the first two group have attained. For those who display opposite characteristics, the reading of Mullā Ṣadrā's commentaries are even juridically forbidden (*harām*).

An excellent example of Mullā Ṣadrā's method of Quranic commentary is to be found in his commentary upon the *āyat al-nūr* which demonstrates the depth of his metaphysical knowledge as well as knowledge of the earlier tradition of sapiential commentary in Islam. At the beginning in his discussion of the meaning of light (*al-nūr*) he writes:

> "God is the light of the heavens and the earth. The similitude of His light is a niche wherein is (a lamp)..."

PREFACE

> "The indication (*ishāra*) regarding the verification (*taḥqīq*) of this verse is prefaced by (our saying) that the word "light" is not--as the veiled ones (*al-*

maḥjūbūn) from among the experts (*'ulamā'*) on language (*lisān*) and theology (*kalām*) understand it--a subject (*mawḍū'*) of the accident (*'araḍ*) which consists of bodies (*ajsām*). They have defined it as a thing which has no duration (*baqā'*) for two moments of time, belonging to created things (*ḥawādith*) which are defective (*nāqiṣa*) in existence. Rather, this light is one of the Names of God the Almighty. He is the one who illuminates the lights, establishes the realities (*ḥaqā'iq*), manifests the ipseities (*huwiyyāt*) and existentiates the quiddites (*māhiyyāt*).

"Light, in its unqualified sense, bears many meanings in vulgar opinion, some of which are homonymous (*bi-al-ishtirāk*), some literal (*bi-al-ḥaqīqa*) and some figurative (*al-majāz*), such as: the light of reason, the light of faith, the light of piety, the light of sapphire, the light of gold, and the light of turquoise.

"In the opinion of the Illuminationists (*al-ishrāqīyīn*) and their followers such as Shaykh al-Maqtūl Shihāb al-Dīn (*al-Suhrawardī*)--the one who unveils their symbols (*rumūz*), extracts their treasures (*kunūz*), records their sciences, sheds light on their understandings (*fuhūm*), exposes their stations (*maqāmāt*), and explains their allusions (*ishārāt*) --(light) is a simple (*basīṭa*) and self-manifesting (*ẓāhira bi-dhātihā*) reality (*ḥaqīqa*), which brings other things to manifestation. Accordingly, (this reality) cannot possess genus (*jins*) or differentia (*faṣl*) because it is not constructed of parts, nor is it made known by definition (*ḥaddī*), nor unveiled by description (*rasmī*), for it is not hidden in itself, rather it is the most manifest (*aẓhar*) of things, since it is the opposite of darkness (*ẓulma*) and hiddenness (*khafā'*), (just as) negation (*salb*) is the opposite of affirmation (*ījāb*). Thus there is no demonstration (*burhān*) for it; rather it is the demonstration for everything.

"Hiddenness and veiling, however, occur (*yaṭra'ān*) to it only according to levels (*marātib*), such as (occurs in the case of) the level of self-subsisting (*qayyūmī*) light--because of its extreme manifestation (*ẓuhūr*) and apparentness (*burūz*). For (what is) intensely manifest and theophanized (*tajallī*) may cause what is manifested to become hidden due to the abundance of (light) and the extreme deficiency of the illuminated thing, just as one observes in the case of bats when strong visible sunlight shines in their pupils. If the situation is thus with regard to sensible light, what would you think about the light of intellect which reaches the peak of intensity and power?

"Light is interpreted by the elder (*akābir*) Sufis according to this meaning, as can be gleaned from their compilations and symbolic tales (*marmūzāt*), although the difference between their school of thought (*madhhab*) and that of the illuminated sages is that light--although it is, according to those elders (Sufis), a simple reality--is exposed, in accordance with its essence (*dhāt*), to variations (*tafāwut*) in intensity and weakness (and exposed to) plurality (*ta'addud*) and multiplicity (*kathra*) in accordance with modes of being (*hay'āt*) and in individualities (*tashakhkhuṣāt*), (as well as exposed to) differences in necessity (*wājibiyya*) and contingency (*mumkiniyya*), substantiality (*jawhariyya*) and accidentality (*'araḍiyya*), independence (*al-ghinā'*) and dependence (*al-iftiqār*).

"As for the opinion of the most erudite noble ones (the illuminated sages), these properties (*aḥkām*) do not occur to it with respect to the definition of its essence, but rather with respect to its theophanies (*tajalliyyāt*), entifications (*ta'ayyunāt*), traits (*shu'ūnāt*) and considerations (*i'tibārāt*). Thus truth is one, and plurality occurs only in accordance with different loci of manifestation (*maẓāhir*), mirrors (*marā'ī*) and receptacles (*qawābil*). It is not unlikely that the difference between the two schools of thought is attributable to their disparity in terminology and ways of alluding to things, their artistry in clarification and intimation and their ways of summarizing and detailing--despite their agreement as far as the foundations and principles are concerned. What Shaykh Muḥammad al-Ghazzālī mentions in the *Mishkāt al-Anwār* when he says, 'Light is an expression by which things are made visible,' is in accord with the statements of the Imams of wisdom.[14]"

* * *

For Mullā Ṣadrā, as for other Islamic esoterists, in the deepest sense the Quran is being (*wujūd*) itself, and his major work on Quranic commentary the *Mafātīḥ al-ghayb*, literally "Keys to the Invisible World" is a key to both the Quran and its complement the world of existence. As expressed by a leading contemporary Persian authority in his introduction to the *Mafātīḥ al-ghayb*:

> "The Quran and being (*wujūd*) are parallel to each other for the Quran issues from the unique and total Name of God and because of its being the theophany of the total Name, reflects all the Divine Names. That is why the *Sharī'ah* of the Quran is the seal of all *Sharī'ahs* and the sanctity (*walāyah*) of the Quran is for the same reason the seal of divine sanctity.[15]
>
> "Like the Quran, being (*wujūd*) possesses letters (*ḥurūf*) which are the keys to the invisible world. From their composition words are made and from their composition verses (*āyāt*)[16] and from their composition chapters. Finally from the (gathering of) chapters the evident book of being with its two aspects of *qur'ān* (gathering) and *furqān* (discernment) is realized. The *furqānī* aspect of the evident book (*kitāb-i mubīn*) is the macrocosm with the total of its details. Its *qur'ānī* and collected (gathered) aspect is the reality of the lordly universal man.
>
> "The lordly Names (*asmā'-i rubūbī*) are the keys to the invisible world and the universal principles of being. And the immutable and unique theophany run through all the great stars as well as in one's children. The science of the Divine Names is the most notable of the sciences and the knowledge of the Prophet and his inerrant family is such a science..."[17]

Shāhrūdī goes on to show the close correspondence between marcrocosmic existence as reflecting various Divine Names and the chapters and verses of the Quran which are also reflections of God's Names and the key to both of these realities through the science of the Names which was possessed by the Prophet and later transmitted to those who are "firm in knowledge."

In fact the very name *Mafātīḥ al-ghayb* was chosen by Mullā Ṣadrā for the work which is the key to his Quranic commentaries because he was seeking "to provide means to gain access to the inner and invisible dimensions of being and of the Quran. For Mullā Ṣadrā, as for many other gnostics and philosophers, the Quran is in complete harmony with being, for it has issued from the Source of being, the Principle of reality and the core of the archetypal world. Therefore, the means which unveil the inner meaning of the Quran also provide an opening toward the inner meaning of being. The key to the invisible aspect of the Quran is also a key to the invisible dimensions of being and vice-versa."[18]

In the *Asfār*, his major philosophical masterpiece and similar works, Mullā Ṣadrā begins with the discussion of *wujūd* and turns from time to time to Quranic verses. In the *Mafātīḥ al-ghayb* and his Quranic commentaries, he begins with the Quran and then turns to the mysteries of *wujūd*. The two types of writing complement each other and reveal the Quranic commentaries of Mullā Ṣadrā as not only journeys into the inner meaning of the Word of God, but also penetrations into the inner dimension of universal existence itself. In these majestic commentaries, so little studied until now outside of Persia and even within the land of Mullā Ṣadrā's birth, one finds one of the most eloquent expositions of not only the meaning of God's revelation in the form of the Word, but also the meaning of that other primordial revelation that is the cosmos and the abode of existence itself.

Notes

1. This fact is reflected in such works as H. Corbin (ed.), *Le Livre des pénétrations métaphysique*, Paris, 1993; Corbin, *En Islam iranien*, vol. IV, Paris, 1971, pp. 54-122; Nasr, *The Islamic Intellectual Tradition in Persia*, London, Curzon Press, 1996; Nasr, "Mullā Ṣadrā", in Nasr and O. Leaman (eds.), *History of Islamic Philosophy*, 2 vols., London, Routledge, 1996, pp. 635-662; F. Rahman, *The Philosophy of Mullā Ṣadrā*, Albany (N.Y.), State University Press of New York, 1976; and J. Morris (ed. and trans.), Mullā, Ṣadrā, *Wisdom of the Throne*, Princeton, Princeton University Press, 1981.

   As for Mullā Ṣadrā's Quranic commentaries practically nothing has been written on the subject in European languages. The essays of L. Peerwani on the subject are a rare exception. See her "Quranic Hermeneutics: The Views of Ṣadr al-Dīn Shīrāzī, "*British Society for Middle East Studies Proceedings*, 1991, pp. 468-477. Also Mullā Ṣadrā's commentary upon the *Āyat al-nūr* (Light Verse) has been translated and analyzed by Muḥsin Ṣāliḥ in a doctoral thesis presented to Temple University in 1993.
2. The fuller title is *Tafsīr al-qur'ān al-karīm ta'līf Ṣadr al-Muta'allihīn*, 7 vols., ed.

M. Khwājawī, Qum, Bīdār Press, 1366, A.H. solar/ 1987-1369/1990.

3. On these traditions of commentary see A. Habil, "Traditional Esoteric Commentaries," in S.H. Nasr (ed.), *Islamic Spirituality-Foundations*, New York, Crossroad Publications, 1987, pp. 24-47.

4. Muḥammad al-Dhahabī, *al-Tafsīr wa'l-mufassirūn*, 2 vols., Cairo, Dār al-Kutub al-Ḥadīth, 1967, vol. I, pp. 89.

5. See G. Böwering. *The Mystical Vision of Existence in Classical Islam: The Quranic Hermeneutics of the Sufi Sahl al-Tustari*, Berlin and New York, de Gruyter, 1980.

6. See M. Chodkiewicz, *An Ocean without Shore, Ibn Arabi, The Book, and the Law*, trans. D. Streight, Albany (N.Y.), State University of New York Press, 1993.

7. We remember that in the 1960's and 70's when 'Allāmah Ṭabāṭabā'ī was writing his al-*Mīzān* commentary, he would often discuss in his weekly meetings with us his reading of Rāzī's commentary concerning the particular chapters and verses with which the 'Allāmah was concerned at that time. He would consider Rāzī's verses carefully before writing his own words without always agreeing with him. Once when we asked him why he considered an Ash'arite commentary so important, he said that although he was an Ash'arite, Rāzī's Quranic commentary contained so much valuable material that it had to be consulted by even those opposed to Ash'arism. As a direct intellectual descendent of Mullā Ṣadrā, 'Allāmah Ṭabāṭabā'ī stated that over the centuries the *ḥukamā-yi ilāhī* of Persia, all of whom opposed Ash'arism philosophically, nevertheless used to consult the *Tafsīr al-kabīr* of Fakhr al-Dīn Rāzī.

8. An exception is L. Gardet in his *La Pensée religieuse d'Avicenne* (Ibn Sīnā), Paris, J. Vrin, 1951, who realized the significance of these commentaries although even in his case the interpretations given are different from those of later followers of Ibn Sīnā in Persia. See also A.F. von Mehren, *Traités mystiques d'Abou Alī al-Husain b. Abdallāh b. Sīnā ou d'Avicenne: texte arabe avec l'explication en français*, Leiden, E.J. Brill, 1889-1891.

9. We follow here the order given by M. Khwājawī in his *Lawāmi' al-'ārifīn fī aḥwāl Ṣadr al-muta'allihīn*, Tehran, Āriyan Press, 1366 A.H. solar/1987, pp. 109ff.

10 As in his philosophical works, so in the Quranic commentaries, Mullā Ṣadrā uses all kinds of gnostic and theosophical terms to designate the chapters of a work, terms such as *mukāshafah, kashf, rukn* and *tasbīḥ*. In this text, however, we have translated all such terms into simply chapters of parts.

11. See above, PP. 39 ff.

12. Usually translated as hermeneutic or esoteric interpretation and commentary, *ta'wīl* means literally to take back something to its origin. Since all things issue from an inward center, to reach the inner meaning of thing means precisely to take things back to that center which is also their origin. To go from the outward *(al-ẓāhir)* to the inward *(al-bāṭin)*, which is how *ta'wīl* has been defined by most traditional masters, is also to return to the Origin from which all that is outward and manifested issues.

13. Mullā Ṣadrā's methodology in commenting upon the Quran has been discussed by M. Khwājawī in his *Lawāmi' al-'ārifīn*, pp. 107 ff.

14. Translated by Muḥsin Ṣāliḥ, *The Verse of Light: A Study of Mullā Ṣadrā's Philosophical Qur'ān Exegesis*, Ph.D. Thesis, Temple University, 1933, pp. 4-9.

15. This doctrine associated with the Muḥammadan Reality as the Logos as such seen within the Islamic universe has been treated by many earlier Sufis especially Ibn 'Arabī. On Ibn 'Arabī's theory of *walāyah/wilāyah* in general see M. Chadkiewicz, *Seal of the Saints-Prophethood and Sainthood in the Doctrine of Ibn 'Arabī*, trans., L. Sherrard, Cambridge, The Islamic Text Society, 1993.

16. It is of the utmost significance to recall here that *āyāt* means both verses of the Quran and phenomena of nature. See S.H. Nasr, *An Introduction to Islamic*

Cosmological Doctrines, Albany (N.Y.), State University of New York Press, 1993, pp. 5 ff.

17. From the introduction of 'Ābidī Shāhrūdī to the *Mafātīḥ al-ghayb* reprinted in Khwājawī, *Lawāmi' al-'ārifīn*, p.202.

18. *Ibid.*, p. 200.

Index

Bibliography on Ṣadr al-Dīn Shīrāzī in European Languages

'Abdul Haq, M., "An Aspect of the Metaphysics of Mullā Ṣadrā", *Islamic Studies,* vol. 9, 1970, pp. 331–53.

——, "The Metaphysics of Mullā Ṣadrā II", *Islamic Studies,* vol. 10, 1971, pp. 291–317.

——, "Mullā Ṣadrā's Concept of Being", *Islamic Studies,* vol. 6, 1967, pp. 268–76.

——, "The Psychology of Mullā Ṣadrā", *Islamic Studies,* vol. 9, 1970, pp. 173–81.

Browne, E.G., *A Literary History of Persia,* vol.m IV, Cambridge, 1969.

Corbin, H. and Āshtiyānī, S.J., *Anthologie des philosophes iraniens,* vol. I, Tehran-Paris, 1972.

——, Corbin, H., *En Islam iranien,* vol. IV, Paris, 1973.

——, Corbin, H., "Histoire de la philosophie islamique, IIe Partie: Depuis la morte d'Averroës jusqu'à nos jours", *Encyclopédie de la Pléiade, Histoire de la philosophie,* IIe partie, Paris, 1974, pp. 1067–88.

——, "La place de Mollā Ṣadrā dans la philosophie iranienne", *Studia Islamica,* vol. XVIII, pp. 81–113.

——, *Le livre des pénétrations métaphysiques,* Tehran-Paris, 1964.

——, "Le thème de la résurrection chez Mollā Ṣadrā Shīrāzī (1050/1640) commentateur de Sohrawardī (587/1191)", in *Studies in Mysticism and Religion presented to Gershom G. Scholem,* Jerusalem, 1967, pp. 71–115.

——, *Terre céleste et corps de résurrection d'aprés quelques traditions iraniennes, Paris, 1961.*

Gobineau, Comte de, *Les religions et les philosophies dans l'Asie Centrale,* Paris, 1923.

Horten, M., *Das philosophische System von Schirazi (1640 †),* Strassburg, 1913.

——, *Die Gottesbeweise bei Schirazi,* Bonn, 1912.

——, *Die Philosophie des Islam,* Munich, 1924.

Iqbal, M., *The Development of Metaphysics in Persia,* London, 1908.

Izutsu, T., *The Concept and Reality of Existence,* Tokyo, 1971.

Nasr, S.H., English introduction to Ṣadr al-Dīn Shīrāzī, *al-Mabda' wa'l-ma'ād* ed. by S.J. Āshtiyānī, Tehran, 1976.

——, English introduction to Ṣadr al-Dīn Shīrāzī, *Three Treatises,* ed. by S.J. Āshtiyānī, Meshed, 1392/1973.

——, English preface to Ṣadr al-Dīn Shīrāzī, *al-Shawāhid al-rubūbiyyah,* ed. by S.J. Āshtiyānī, Meshed, 1967.

——, "Mullā Ṣadrā and the Doctrine of the Unity of Being", *Philosophical Forum,* vol. IV, no. 1, Fall, 1972, pp. 153–61.

——, "Mullā Ṣadrā as a Source for the History of Muslim Philosophy", *Islamic Studies,* vol. III, no. 3, Sept., 1964, pp. 309–14.

——, (ed.), *Mullā Ṣadrā Commemoration Volume,* Tehran, 1380/1961.

——, "Mullā Ṣadrā" in *The Encyclopedia of Philosophy,* vol. 5, New York, 1966, pp. 411–13.

——, "Ṣadr al-Dīn Shīrāzī, His Life, Doctrine and Significance", *Indo-Iranica,* vol. XIV, no. 4, Dec. 1961, pp. 6–16.

——, "Ṣadr al-Dīn Shīrāzi 'Mullā Ṣadrā' ", in Sharif, M.M., (ed.), *A History of Muslim Philosophy,* vol. II, Wiesbaden, 1966, pp. 932–61.

Rahman, Fazlur, "The Eternity of the World and the Heavenly Bodies in Post-Avicennian Philosophy", in Hourani, G. (ed.), *Essays on Islamic Philosophy and Science,* Albany (New York), 1975, pp. 322–37.

——, "The God-World Relationship in Mullā Ṣadrā", in Hourani, G., (ed.), *Essays on Islamic Philosophy and Science,* Albany (New York), 1975, pp. 238–53.

——, "Mullā Ṣadrā's Theory of Knowledge", *Philosophical Forum,* vol. IV, no. 1, Fall, 1972, pp. 141–52.

——, *The Philosophy of Mullā Ṣadrā,* Albany (New York), 1976.

Sabahuddin, Abdur Rahman, "Mullā Ṣadrā", *Indo-Iranica,* vol. XIV, no. 4, Dec. 1961, pp. 17–29.

Yusuf, K.M., "Iran Society celebrates the Quadrincenary of Mullā Ṣadrā", *Indo-Iranica,* vol. XIV, no. 4, Dec. 1961, pp. 1–5.

Supplementary Bibliography (1977-1997) on Ṣadr al-Dīn Shīrāzī in European Languages

Açikgenç, A., *Being and Existence in Ṣadrā and Heidgger*, Kuala Lumpur, International Institute of Islamic Thought and Civilization, 1993.

Corbin, H., *Le livre des pénétrations métaphysiques*, Paris, Verdier, 1988.

Ha'iri Yazdi, M., *The Principles of Epistemology in Islamic Philosophy – Knowledge by Presence*, Albany, State University of New York Press, 1992.

Morris, J. (ed. and trans.), *The Wisdom of the Throne*, Princeton, Princeton University Press, 1981.

Nasr, S.H., *Islamic Life and Thought*, Albany, State University of New York Press, 1981.

Nasr, S.H., "Mullā Ṣadrā: his teachings", in S.H. Nasr and O. Leaman (eds.), *History of Islamic Philosophy*, London, Routledge, vol. 2, 1996, pp. 643 - 62.

Peerwani, L., "Quranic Hermeneutics: The Views of Ṣadr al-Dīn Shīrāzī", *British Society for Middle East Studies Proceedings*, 1991, pp. 468 - 77.

Ziai, H., "Mullā Ṣadrā: his life and works", in S.H. Nasr and O.Leaman (eds.), *History of Islamic of Philosophy*, London, Routledge, vol. 2, 1996, pp. 635-42.

Other Works by the Authour in European languages

Mullā Ṣadrā Commemoration Volume. (E&P) (ed.) Tehran: Tehran, University Press. 1961.

Introduction to Islamic Cosmological Doctrines. Preface by H.A.R. Gibb. Cambridge: Harvard University Press, 1964. Second edition, New York and London: Thames and Hudson, 1978. Paperback edition, Boulder: Shambhala, ·1978. New edition, Albany: State University of New York Press, 1992.

Three Muslim Sages. Preface R.H.L. Slater. Cambridge: Harvard University Press, 1964. Second printing, 1969. Reprinted, Delmar: Caravan Book, 1976, 1986. Reprinted, Lahore: Suhail Academy, 1988; Bosnian-Serbo-Croation translation as *Tri Muslimanska Mudraca*. Trans. Becir Dzaka. Sarajevo: El-Kalem, 1991.

L'Histoire de la Philosophic Islamique. Collaboration with H. Corbin and O. Yahya. Vol. 1. Paris: Gallimard (collection idees), 1964. (collection folio/essais), 1986; English translation as *History of Islamic Philosophy*. Trans. Liadain Sherrard. London: Routledge and Kegan Paul, 1993; Italian translation as *Storia della filosofia Islamica*. Collaboration with H. Corbin and O. Yahya. Trans. Vanna Calasso. Milan: Adelphia edizioni, 1973; Bosinan-Serbo-Croation translation as *Historija Islamske filosofije*. Trans. Nerkes Smailagie and Tarik Haveric. Sarejevo: Biblioteka Logos, 1987; Spanish translation as *Historia de la filosofia: Del mundo romano al Islam medieval*. Madrid: Siglo XXI Editores, 1972, Sixth edition, 1984.

Iran (Reading Material for Use in Teaching about Eastern Cultures). Paris: UNESCO, 1966. Reprinted, Tehran: Pahlavi Library, 1971. Tehran: Offset Press, 1973; French translation as *Iran* (Document à utiliser pour l'enseignement des cultures orientales). Paris: UNESCO, 1966. Reprinted, Tehran: Pahlavi Library, 1971. Tehran: Offset Press, 1973.

Ideals and Realities of Islam. London: Allen and Unwin, 1966, 1975. Preface by Huston Smith. Boston: Beacon Press, 1972. Paperback edition, 1979, 1985, 1988. Karachi: Haider Ali Muljee Tahal (n.d). Cairo: The American University of Cairo Press, 1989; Italian translation as *Ideali e realtà dell'Islam*. Trans. Donatella Venturi. Milan: Rusconi editore, 1974. Second edition, 1989; French translation as *Islam, perspectives et réalités*.Trans. H. Crès. Preface by T. Burckhardt. Paris: Buchet-Chastel, 1975. Second edition, 1978. Third edition, 1992; Polish Translation as *Idee i Wartosci Ismanu. Trans.* Janusz Danecki. Warszawa: Intytut Wydawnizy Pax, 1988; German translation as *Ideal und Wirklichkeit des Islam*. Trans. Clemens Williams. Munich: Diederichs Gelbe Reihe, 1993.

Islamic Studies: Essays on law and Society, the Sciences, Philosophy and Sufism. Beirut: Librate du Liban, 1967.

Science and Civilization in Islam. Preface by G. de Santillana. Cambridge: Harvard University Press, 1968. New York: New American Library, 1970. New York, London and Toronto: Mentor Classics, 1970. Lahore: Suhail Academy, 1983. Kuala Lumpur: Dewan Pustaka Fajar, 1984. Second edition, Cambridge: Islamic Text Society, 1987. New York: Barnes and Noble, 1992; Italian translation as *Scienza e civiltà nell'Islam.* Trans. Libero Sosio. Milano: Giangiacomo Feltrinelli, 1977; French translation as *Sciences et savoir en Islam.* Trans. Jean-Pierre Guinhut. Paris: Sinbad, 1979. Second edition, Paris: Sinbad, 1992.

The Encounter of Man and Nature: The Spiritual Crisis of Modern Man. London: Allen and Unwin, 1968. Reprinted with an additional preface as *Man and Nature.* London: Unwin Paperbacks, 1976. Kuala Lumpur: Foundation for Traditional Studies, 1986. New edition, London: Unwin and Hyman and Harper-Collins, 1990; Italian translation as *L'Homo e la natura: la crisi spirituale dell'uomo moderno.* Trans. Giorgio Spina. Milan: Rusconi, 1977; Portuguese translation as *O Homem e a Natureza.* Trans. Raul Bezzerra Pedreira Filho. Rio de Janeiro: Zahar Editores, 1977; French translation as *L'Homme face à la nature: la crise spirituelle de l'homme moderne.* Trans. Gisele Kondracki and Jeanine Loreau. Paris: Buchet-Chastel, 1978; Spanish translation as *Hombre y naturaleza.* Trans. Hetor Morel. Buenos Aires: Editorial Kier, 1982; Bosnian-Serbo-Croation translation as *Susre covjeka I prirode.* Trans. Enes Karić, Svjetlost, Sarajevo: 1992.

Historical Atlas of Iran. Edited with others and introduction in English, French and Persian. Tehran: Tehran University Press, 1971.

Sufi Essays. London: Allen and Unwin, 1972. Albany: State University of New York Press, 1973. Paperback edition, New York: Schocken Books, 1977. *As Living Sufism.* London: Allen and Unwin, 1980. Albany: State University of New York Press, 1985. Second edition, Albany: State University of New York Press, 1991; Italian translation as *Il Sufismo.* Trans. Donatella Venturi. Milan: Rusconi editore, 1989; French translation as *Essais sur le soufisme.* Trans. Jean Herbert. Paris: Albin Michel, 1980; Spanish translation as *Sufismo vivo: Ensayos sobre la dimensión esotérica del Islam.* Trans. F. Blanch and E. Serra. Barcelona: Herder, 1985.

al-Bīrūnī: An Annotated Bibliography. Tehran: High Council of Culture and the Arts, 1973.

Jalāl al-Dīn Rūmī: Supreme Persian Poet and Sage. Tehran: High Council of

Culture and the Arts, 1974.

Shi'ite Islam, by 'Allāmah Ṭabāṭabā'ī. Trans. from the Persian and edited with introduction and notes. Albany: State University of New York Press, 1975. London: Allen and Unwin, 1975; Second edition, 1977; Paperback edition, 1979.

With R. Beny. *Persia: Bridge of Turquoise*. Toronto: MC Clelland and Stewart, 1975. London: Thames and Hudson, 1975. New York: Times and Life, 1975; French translation as *la Perse: pont de turquoise*, Fonds Mercator. Hatier: 1976; German translation as *Persien*. Luzern: Bucher, c1976; Italian translation as *Persia: un ponte di turchese*. Milano: Arnoldo Mondadori Editore, 1977, c1976.

With W. Chittick. *An Annotated Bibliography of Islamic Science. Vol. I*. Tehran: Iranian Academy of Philosophy, 1975. Second edition, Lahore: Suhail Academy, 1985.

With W. Chittick and Peter Zirnis. *An Annotated Bibliography of Islamic Science. Vol. II*. Tehran: Iranian Academy of Philosophy, 1978. Second edition, Lahore: Suhail Academy, 1985.

With W. Chittick. *An Annotated Bibliography of Islamic Science. Vol. III*. Tehran: Mu'assisa-yi muṭāli'ā'āt wa taḥqīqāt, 1991.

Islam and the Plight of Modern Man. London. Longmans, 1976. Kuala Lumpur: Foundation for Traditional Studies, 1987. Lahore: Suhail Academy, 1988.

Islamic Science: An Illustrated Study. London: World of Islam Festival Trust, 1976.

Western Science and Asian Cultures. New Delhi: Indian Council for Cultural Relations, 1976. Lahore: Iqbal Academy, 1985.

Islamic Life and Thought. London: Allen and Unwin, 1981. Albany: State University of New York Press, 1981. Lahore: Suhail Academy, 1985; Spanish translation as *Vida y pensamiento en el Islam*. Trans. Esteve Serra. Barcelona: Herder, 1985.

Knowledge and the Sacred. New York: Crossroad, 1981. Lahore: Suhail Academy, 1988. Reprinted as hard cover and paperback, Albany: State University of New York Press, 1989; German translation as *Die Erkenntnis und das Heilige*. Trans. Clemens Wilhelm. Munich: Eugen Diederichs Verlag, 1990; French translation as *La Connaissance et le sacré*. Trans. Patrick Laude. Paris: L'Age d'Homme, 1997.

Philosophy, Literature and Fine Arts: Islamic Education Series. Kent: Hodder and Stoughton, 1982.

The Essential Writings of Frithjof Schuon. (ed.) Warwick: Amity House, 1986. Paperback edition, Rockport: Element Books, 1991.

Islamic Art and Spirituality. London: Golgonooza Press, 1987. Albany: State University of New York, 1987. Delhi: Indira Gandhi National Center for the Arts, 1990.

Traditional Islam in the Modern World. London and New York: KPT, 1987; Paperback edition, 1990. Kuala Lumpur: Foundation for Traditional Studies, 1989; French translation as *L'Islam traditional face au monde moderne.* Trans. G. Kondracki. Paris: L'Age d'Homme, 1993; Bosnian-Serbo-Croation translation as *Tradicionalni Islam U Modernom Svijetu.* Trans. Enes Karić and others, Sarajevo: 1994.

Islamic Spirituality: Foundations. (ed.) Vol. 19 of World Spirituality: An Encyclopedic History of the Religious Quest. New York: Crossroad Publications, 1987; London: Routledge and Kegan Paul, 1992.

Muhammad: Man of Allah. London: Muhammadi Trust, 1982; Reprinted, 1988. New edition as *Muhammad: Man of God.* Chicago: Kazi Publication, 1995.

Shi'ism: Doctrines, Thought and Spirituality. (ed.) with H. Dabashi and S.V.R. Nasr Albany: State University of New York Press, 1988.

Expectation of the Millenium: Shi'ism in History. (ed.) with H. Dabashi and S.V.R. Nasr. Albany: State University of New York Press, 1989.

Islamic Spirituality: Manifestations. (ed.) Vol. 20 of *World Spirituality: An Encyclopedic History of the Religious Quest.* New York: Crossroad Publications, 1991. London: Routledge and Kegan Paul, 1992.

Religion and Religions: The Challenge of Living in a Multireligious World. The Roy H. Witherspoon Lectures in Religious Studies, The University of North Carolina at Charlotte, April 8, 1985. Charlotte: 1991.

Religion of the Heart: Essays to Frithjof Schuon on his Eightieth Birthday. (ed.) with W. Stoddart. Washington D.C.: Foundation for Traditional Studies, 1991.

The Need for a Sacred Science. Albany: State University of New York Press, 1993.

In Quest of the Sacred Science. (ed.) with K. O'Brien. Albany: State University of New York Press, 1993.

The Young Muslim's Guide to the Modern World. Chicago: Kazi Publications, 1993; Cambridge: Islamic Text Society, 1994.

History of Islamic Philosophy. (ed.) with O. Leaman. London: Routledge, 1996.

The Islamic Intellectual Tradition in Persia. (ed.) M. Aminrazavi. London: Curzon Press, 1996.

Religion and the Order of Nature. London: Oxford University Press, 1996.

CPSIA information can be obtained
at www.ICGtesting.com
Printed in the USA
JSHW052319030622
26637JS00001B/75

9 789644 260346